FREEDOM TO RO

The North York Moors

The North York Moors

Judy Armstrong

Series editor Andrew Bibby

FRANCES LINCOLN

The Ramblers

FREEDOM TO ROAM

The Freedom to Roam guides
are dedicated to the memory of
Benny Rothman

Frances Lincoln Ltd
4 Torriano Mews
Torriano Avenue
London NW5 2RZ
www.franceslincoln.com

First published by Frances Lincoln 2006

British Library Cataloguing in Publication Data
A catalogue record for this book is available from the British Library

ISBN 0-7112-2556-7
Printed and bound in Singapore by Kyodo Printing Co.
9 8 7 6 5 4 3 2 1

Frontispiece photograph: In the heart of the North York Moors near Danby

Contents

Before you go – a checklist

- *Are access-land restrictions in place?*
  Access land may be subject to temporary or permanent restrictions. Check at www.countrysideaccess.gov.uk or on 0845 100 3298.

- *Are weather conditions appropriate?*
  When poor weather is forecast, it may be sensible to postpone some of the walks in this book.

- *Do you have suitable equipment?*
  High ground can be significantly colder and more exposed than valley areas. A map and compass are recommended.

- *Does someone know where you are going?*
  If walking in a remote area, it is a good idea to leave details of your route and time of return.

- *Do you want to take a dog?*
  In general, you should assume that you will *not* be able to take dogs on open country. Most of the moors covered by this book have dog-exclusion orders in place. Check on the website or helpline given above.

- *Are birds nesting?*
  Between March and June open country is home to many ground-nesting birds. To find out where conservation restrictions are in force, check on the website or helpline given above.

Acknowledgements

The author gratefully acknowledges the assistance given to her by the following individuals: Duncan Macdonald, Sylvia Bernard, Suzy Grindley (Open Access Officer, North York Moors National Park) and Emma Farley (Countryside Interpretation, North York Moors National Park).

Series introduction

This book, and the companion books in the series, celebrate the arrival in England and Wales of the legal right to walk in open country. The title for the series is borrowed from a phrase much used during the long campaign for this right – Freedom to Roam. For years, it was the dream of many to be able to walk at will across mountain top, moorland and heath, free of the risk of being confronted by a 'Keep Out' sign or being turned back by a gamekeeper.

The sense of frustration that the hills were, in many cases, out of bounds to ordinary people was captured in the song 'The Manchester Rambler' written by one of the best-known figures in Britain's post-war folk revival, Ewan MacColl. The song, which was inspired by the 1932 'mass trespass' on Kinder Scout when walkers from Sheffield and Manchester took to the forbidden Peak District hills, tells the tale of an encounter between a walker, trespassing on open land, and an irate gamekeeper:

He called me a louse, and said 'Think of the grouse',
Well I thought but I still couldn't see
Why old Kinder Scout, and the moors round about,
Couldn't take both the poor grouse and me.

The desire, as Ewan MacColl expressed it, was a simple one:

So I'll walk where I will, over mountain and hill
And I'll lie where the bracken is deep,
I belong to the mountains, the clear running fountains
Where the grey rocks rise ragged and steep.

Some who loved the outdoors and campaigned around the time of the Kinder Scout trespass in the 1930s must have thought that the legal right to walk in open country would be won after the Second World War, at the time when the national parks were being created and the rights-of-way network drawn up. It was not to be. It was another half century before, finally, Parliament passed the Countryside and Rights of Way Act 2000, and the people of England and Wales gained the legal right to take to the hills and the moors. (Scotland has its own traditions and its own legislation.)

We have dedicated this series to the memory of Benny Rothman, one of the leaders of the 1932 Kinder Scout mass trespass who was imprisoned for his part in what was deemed a 'riotous assembly'. Later in his life, Benny Rothman was a familiar figure at rallies called by the Ramblers' Association as once again the issue of access rights came to the fore. But we should pay tribute to all who have campaigned for this goal. Securing greater access to the countryside was one of the principles on which the Ramblers' Association was founded in 1935, and for many ramblers the access legislation represents the achievement of literally a lifetime of campaigning.

So now, at last, we do have freedom to roam. For the first time in several centuries, the open mountains, moors and heaths of England and Wales are open for all. We have the protected right to get our boots wet in the peat bogs, to flounder in the tussocks, to blunder and scrabble through the bracken and heather, and to discover countryside which, legally, we had no way of knowing before.

The Freedom to Roam series of books has one aim: to encourage you to explore and grow to love these new areas of the countryside which are now open to us. The right to roam freely – that's surely something to celebrate.

Andrew Bibby

Walking in open country – a guide to using this book

If the right and the freedom to roam openly are so important – perceptive readers may be asking – why produce a set of books to tell you where to go?

So a word of explanation about this series. The aim is certainly not to encourage walkers to follow each other, ant-like, over the hills, sticking rigidly to a pre-determined itinerary. We are not trying to be prescriptive, instructing you on your walk stile by stile or gate by gate. The books are not intended as instruction manuals but we hope that they will be valuable as *guides* – helping you discover areas of the countryside which you haven't legally walked on before, advising you on routes you might want to take and telling you about places of interest you will be passing along the way.

In areas where it can be tricky to find routes or track down landmarks, we offer more detailed instructions. Elsewhere, we are deliberately less precise in our directions, allowing you to choose your own particular path or line to follow. For each walk, however, there is a recommended core route, and this forms the basis on which the distances given are calculated.

There is, then, an assumption that those who use this book will be comfortable with using a map – and that, in practice, means one of the Ordnance Survey's 1:25 000 Explorer series of maps. As well as referring to the maps in this book, it is worth taking the full OS map with you, to give you a wider picture of the countryside you will be exploring.

Safety in the hills

Those who are already experienced upland walkers will not be surprised if at this point we put in a note on basic safety in the hills. Walkers need to remember that walking in open country, particularly high country, is different from footpath walking across farmland or more gentle countryside. The main risk for walkers is of being inadequately prepared for changes in the weather. Even in high summer, hail and even snow are not impossible. Daniel Defoe found this out in August 1724 when he crossed the Pennines from Rochdale, leaving a calm clear day behind to find himself almost lost in a blizzard on the tops.

If rain comes the temperature will drop as well, so it is important to be properly equipped when taking to the hills and to guard against hypothermia. Fortunately, walkers today have access to a range of wind- and rain-proof clothing which was not available in the eighteenth century. Conversely, in hot weather you should take sufficient water to avoid the risk of dehydration and hyperthermia (dangerous overheating of the body).

Be prepared for visibility to drop when (to use the local term) the clag descends on the hills. It is always sensible to take a compass. If you are unfamiliar with basic compass-and-map work, ask in a local outdoor equipment shop whether they have simple guides available or pick the brains of a more experienced walker.

The other main hazard, even for walkers who know the hills well, is that of suffering an accident such as a broken limb. If you plan to walk alone, it is sensible to let someone know in advance where you will be walking and when you expect to be back – the moorland and mountain rescue services which operate in the area covered by this book are very experienced but they are not psychic. Groups of walkers should tackle only what the least experienced or least fit member of the party can comfortably achieve. Take particular care if you intend to take children with you to hill country. And take a mobile phone by all means, but don't assume you can rely on it in an emergency, since some parts of the moors and hills will not pick up a signal. (If you can make a call and are in a real emergency situation, ring 999 – it is the police who co-ordinate mountain and moorland rescues.)

If this all sounds off-putting, that is certainly not the intention. The guiding principle behind the access legislation is that walkers will exercise their new-won rights with responsibility. Taking appropriate safety precautions is simply one aspect of acting responsibly.

Access land – what you can and can't do

The countryside which is covered by access legislation includes mountain, moor, heath, downland and common land. After the passing of the Countryside and Rights of Way Act 2000, a lengthy mapping process was undertaken, culminating in the production of 'conclusive' maps which identify land which is open for access. These maps (although not intended as guides for walking) can be accessed via the Internet, at www.countrysideaccess.gov.uk. Ordnance Survey maps

Note: Each walk has been graded, on a scale of 👢 to 👢👢👢👢, for the degree of difficulty involved. In general, walks are judged more difficult if they are (a) longer in mileage, and/or (b) involve more rough walking (across open moorland rather than on established footpaths), and/or (c) pose more navigational problems or venture into very unfrequented areas. But bear in mind that all the walks in this book require map-reading competence and some experience of hill walking.

published from 2004 onwards also show access land.

You can walk, run, birdwatch and climb on access land, although there is no right to camp or to bathe in streams or lakes (or, of course, to drive vehicles). The regulations sensibly insist that dogs, where permitted, are on leads near livestock and during the bird-nesting season (1 March–31 July). However, grouse moors have the right to ban dogs altogether and they are indeed excluded from most heather moorland in the North York Moors. This means that you should assume that you will not be able to take dogs with you for the

walks in this book. (For more information, watch for local signs.)

Access legislation also does not include the right to ride horses or bikes, though in some areas there may be pre-existing agreements that allow this. More information is available on the website given above and, the at time of writing, there is an advice line on 0845 100 3298.

The access legislation allows for some open country to be permanently excluded from the right to roam. 'Excepted' land includes military land, quarries and areas close to buildings, and in addition landowners can apply for other open land to be excluded.

Fat Betty at sunset

To the best of the authors' knowledge, all the walks in the Freedom to Roam series are either on legal rights of way or across access land included in the official 'conclusive' maps. However, you are asked to bear in mind that the books have been produced right at the start of the new access arrangements, before walkers have begun to walk the hills regularly and before any teething problems on the ground have been ironed out. As access becomes better established, it may be that minor changes to the routes suggested in these books will become appropriate or necessary. You are asked to remember that we are encouraging you to be flexible in the way you use the guides.

Walkers in open country also need to be aware that landowners have a further right to suspend or restrict access to their land for up to twenty-eight days a year. (In such cases of temporary closure there is normally still access on public holidays and on most weekends.) Notice of closure needs to be given in advance and the plan is that this information should be readily available to walkers, it is hoped at local information centres and libraries and also on the countryside access website and at popular entry points to access land. This sort of set-up has generally worked well in Scotland, where arrangements have been made to ensure that walkers in areas where deer hunting takes place can find out when and where hunting is happening.

Walkers will understand the sense in briefly closing small areas of open countryside when, for example, shooting is in progress (grouse shooting begins on 12 August) or when heather burning is taking place in spring. Once again, however, it is too early in the implementation of the access legislation to know how easily walkers in England and Wales will be able to find out about these temporary access closures. It is also too early to know whether landowners will attempt to abuse this power.

In some circumstances, additional restrictions on access can be introduced – for example, on the grounds of nature or heritage conservation, following the advice of English Nature or English Heritage.

Bear these points in mind, but enjoy your walking in the knowledge that any access restrictions should be the exception and not the norm. If you find access unexpectedly denied while walking in the areas suggested in this book, please accept the restrictions and follow the advice you are given. However, if you feel that access was wrongly denied, please report your experience to the countryside service of the local authority (or national park authority, in national park areas) and to the Ramblers' Association.

Finally, there may be occasions when you choose voluntarily not to exercise your freedom to roam. For example, many of the upland moors featured in these books are the homes of ground-nesting birds such as grouse, curlew, lapwing and pipit, who will be nesting in spring and early summer. During this time, many people will decide to leave the birds in peace and find other places to walk. Rest assured that you will know if you are approaching an important nesting area – birds are good at telling you that they would like you to go away.

Celebrating the open countryside

Despite these necessary caveats, the message from this series is, we hope, clear. Make the most of the new legal rights we have been given – and enjoy your walking.

Andrew Bibby

Introduction

Draw a wobbly line from Scarborough to Thirsk through the country where James Herriot lived and worked, continue up over the Cleveland Hills to Captain Cook's patch at Staithes, then scribble a ragged edge down the coast to join up the circle. Inside that ring, made famous by vet and explorer, is the wild heart of North Yorkshire.

Hidden valleys with daffodil carpets and sturdy stone villages are split by great expanses of moorland. High on the wild plateau, stone crosses hide their runes with bracken, and heather explodes purple over ancient burial mounds. In winter the high roads are impassable when heavy snow falls, and the moors become difficult places where navigation is a vital art. But in summer, when the sun beats down on the green dales and purple uplands, when the air is heavy with the tangy smell of heather and wild garlic, walkers stride freely through empty, open spaces.

Open, yes, but not untravelled. Humans have lived on the North York Moors for centuries and the uplands and valleys are laced with some 1433 miles (2307 kilometres) of footpaths and bridleways. One of Britain's best long-distance trails, Wainwright's Coast to Coast Walk from St Bee's Head to Robin Hood's Bay, traverses these moors. The Cleveland Way and its Link extension, together totalling 157 miles (255 kilometres), loop around them, and the 35-mile (56-kilometre) Esk Valley Walk wanders over the lofty moorland and down to the coast at Whitby.

The coast is famous in its own right; recognized as an exceptional undeveloped land- and seascape, it was designated as a Heritage Coast in 1974 (Walk 11). Much of the cliff face and rocky shore has also been named as a Site of Special Scientific Interest (SSSI) by English Nature. Rugged headlands, deep bays and golden beaches are crucial elements, with footpaths on the crumbling cliff tops and fossils, including a recently discovered sea dragon, at their bases.

The coastline that borders the eastern fringe of the North York Moors is an important part of the area's attraction for many walkers. Raw, windswept and exhilarating as it is, the coastline is not, however, the main focus of this book. Instead it's the heathery heights, averaging around 1000 feet (300 metres) above sea level, that will feature most. The upland moors are visible from miles around; from almost any direction, but particularly from the south and west, the approaching visitor will see an escarpment rising into the sky.

Rising sharply from the plains, the Hambleton Hills, Cleveland Hills and Tabular Hills (Walks 4 and 5) are characterized by exposed cliffs, deep gorges formed by glacial run-offs and sloping, almost flat, tops. There are no rugged mountains here; instead, you will find numerous long, airy ridges where views across the north of England give a feeling of altitude and space. These ridges often have roads along their spines, but these man-made tracks somehow fail to impose on the landscape. They are arteries feeding the whole, and a way on to the moorland.

Ah, the moorland. As anyone who has ever picked up a book on North Yorkshire knows, the North York Moors contain the largest expanse of heather moorland in England and Wales. From early July the bright bell heather bursts into bloom, soon followed by the paler, cross-leafed heath. From mid-August vast swathes of the moorland turn purple as ling, or common heather, comes into flower.

This display of colour is not for the benefit of walkers; it is a result of the management of moorland for the heather-loving red grouse. Gamekeepers and moorkeepers play a fundamental part in conserving the North York Moors and in controlling the rats, foxes, stoats and weasels that prey on moorland birds. Of course, there is more to the moors than the commercial aspects of grouse: the heather is also an essential habitat for an impressive array of fauna, from the delicate merlin, Britain's smallest raptor, to the golden plover and basking adder.

Heather is the most obvious and prolific plant but bilberry, wavy hair grass and bog plants also enliven the moorland. This diversity has been recognized by English Nature: since 2000 110,000 acres, nearly a third of the national park, have been designated an SSSI for the heathland and bird-breeding habitats to be found there.

While heather and merlin may be part of the 'pretty' picture, the area's appeal is also based on thoroughly tangible attractions. The North York Moors boast a working steam railway (Walk 10), houses with witch posts (page 152), an ancient church dating back to 654 (Walk 2) and Whitby Abbey, where Dracula is said to have plotted and schemed. Ruined castles, Roman roads, relics of the former ironstone and jet industries and an unrivalled collection of wayside crosses, some bearing ancient Christian symbols and others serving as waymarks or boundary stones, are here for the finding.

The moors are also familiar to millions through television and cinema. The moorland village of Goathland, for example, is better known to the British public through the television series *Heartbeat*, and the North York Moors steam railway that serves it is famous from the Harry Potter films.

These latter-day influences are part of the landscape, but have played no role in shaping it. That job went in part to the mining industries, which had a significant hand in creating the moors we see today. Alum, iron, coal and jet were sought after, and stone and sand were quarried. At first they were moved out to market by packhorses, often using the old pannier tracks across the moor (page 96). By the mid-nineteenth century railways had punched across the uplands, transporting the ore to more accessible pick-up points for distribution throughout the country (page 31). This had a dramatic effect on the development of villages in valleys like Rosedale, in the central moorlands, and along the line of the Cleveland Extension Mineral Railway, which runs across the moor's northern edge.

The mining industry had a significant impact but, as so often with man's interventions, it was temporary. Beneath the feet of the miners, beyond the reach of the iron industry, lay the landscape's unique geological heart.

This is truly a Jurassic park: the rocks beneath the heather are around 150 million years old. Even earlier, over 200 million years ago, great rivers flowed down from the north, creating sand banks and swamps which nurtured plant life that in turn sustained a community of animals, dominated by dinosaurs. While dinosaur bones are rare here, their footprints are relatively common and are among the most important fossils of the area.

The region has been flooded by oceans, covered by huge river deltas and invaded by ice sheets, but the scenery we see now was not simply shaped by natural forces. As well as the mining industries, agriculture has played a crucial role in creating the North York Moors as they are today. About 5000 years ago the moors were covered with forest, but for centuries they have been grazed by sheep and these days sheep farming and management for grouse shooting maintain the landscape.

Evidence of human interaction with this place dates back to the last Ice Age, which ended about 10,000 years ago. Early farmers left their mark all over the moors, seen most easily in the stony mounds that were clearance cairns, and boundary banks. Major archaeological investigations have revealed a massive hill fort, believed to date from 400 BC, at Roulston Scar at Sutton Bank, near Thirsk. Covering an area of 60 acres and defended by a perimeter over 1 mile (2 kilometres) long, this is the largest Iron Age fort of its kind in the north of England.

Later, Christianity had a hand in shaping the moors. The abbeys, priories and monasteries, most famously Rievaulx and Byland, continue to be focal points for visitors, but traditionally the upland was also a scene of religious activity. The earliest foundation was made in 1131 through a grant of land at Rievaulx to a group of Cistercian monks from France, and by the sixteenth century nearly a third of the land within what is now the national park was under the direct control of monasteries.

The monks were successful farmers, developing large-scale moorland grazing and stimulating the growth of the wool trade. Many of the stone-flagged tracks that form networks on the moors are known as monks' trods, used by the religious orders to move their goods from the heather upland to the coast.

While the monks, and before them the Roman, Viking and Anglo-Saxon farmers, may have created the landscapes, agriculture remains a fundamental part of life on the North York Moors. Sheep are, of course, the traditional agricultural mainstay, but today we see an element of diversification. A handful of organic farmers, for example, are producing high-quality meat, fruit, vegetables, breads and juices; one is even manufacturing tools to deal with bracken, the scourge of moorland farmers, without recourse to chemicals. In some moorland communities renewable-energy teams have been created to investigate energy consumption, monitor carbon dioxide emissions and develop alternative sources such as wind and water power.

Moorland villages continue to thrive. Winter nights are cheered by dominoes in the local pubs, by darts and pool tournaments. In summer, a flurry of agricultural and produce shows punctuate the week. Children hang breathlessly over the ferrets' towers to see which furry face will emerge first, and prized pets parade under the eagle eyes of smartly coiffured judges. Competition is fierce indeed; who grows the biggest onion matters in these parts.

It is this sense of tradition and community that attracts many walkers to the North York Moors. Once here, they are spoilt for choice: the North York Moors National Park, formed in 1952, covers an area of nearly 550 square miles (1425 square kilometres). Efforts are being made to provide adequate public transport throughout the park and the Moorsbus (see page 77), which weaves an elaborate web over the moors in summer, provides an essential service for many walkers.

With the help of the Moorsbus public-transport system, the national park's superb infrastructure and the sheer diversity of terrain, walkers will find that they can cast their net wide. The national park authority has taken an extremely proactive stance in opening access, with around seventy information signboards being erected at key moorland access points. Walkers now have access to about 47 per cent of the North York Moors countryside.

Conscious of the fact that the open access land is home to many species of ground-nesting birds, the park authority is contributing data to a national programme which monitors the impact of the access arrangements on wildlife. As a result, local restrictions may be in place during sensitive times, such as the bird-nesting season between March and July, and on certain grouse moors in August.

More voluntary rangers have been recruited to assist walkers and explain any access restrictions, bringing the total number of rangers in the park to more than two hundred. These men and women, who walk the park for the love of the place, are eager to share their knowledge and enthusiasm. They know, as do the walkers who already enjoy the North York Moors, that the existing web of footpaths and bridleways covers many areas of outstanding beauty and interest. And with the addition, through the open access legislation, of estate tracks, ancient trails and open moorland, there are now even more ways in which these wonderful moors can be enjoyed.

WALK 1

VIEWS AND CROSSES

DIFFICULTY (2 boots) **or** (3 boots) **depending on height of heather on untracked sections**

DISTANCE 5¾ miles (9.3 km)

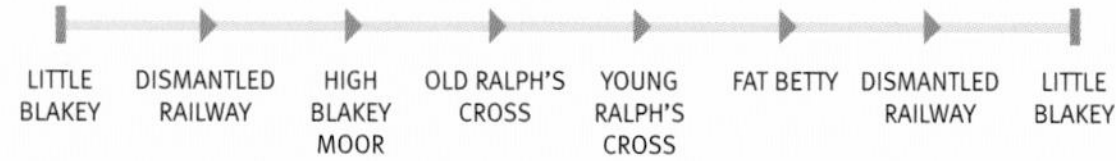

MAP OS Explorer OL26, North York Moors (Western Area)

STARTING POINT Little Blakey/Farndale Bank Top, south of the Lion Inn on Blakey Ridge (GR 683989)

PUBLIC TRANSPORT Moorsbus M1, M3 (see page 77). Ask to be let off at Little Blakey.

PARKING Cleared areas on either side of the road at the starting point

A short walk with views into four valleys (Farndale, Westerdale, Danby Dale and Rosedale) and out to the sea. The route utilizes the dismantled Rosedale railway line but also crosses untracked moorland, so please pay attention to ground-nesting birds. They are particularly vulnerable from March to June.

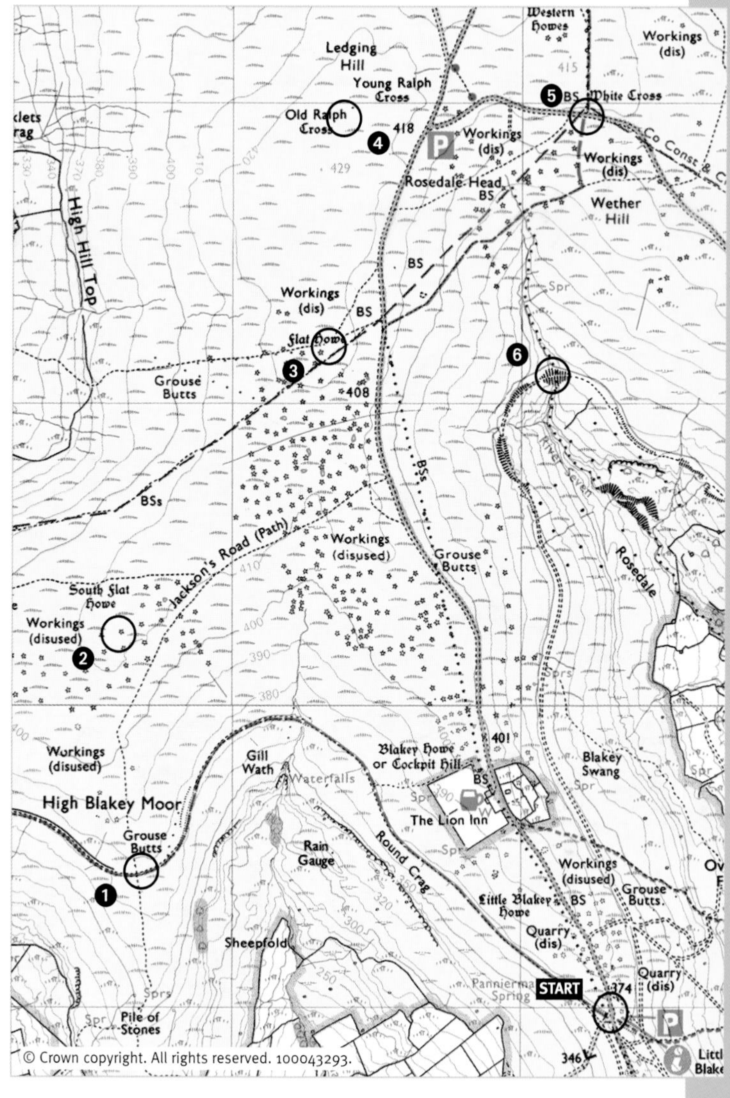
Western Howes
Workings (dis)
Ledging Hill
415
Young Ralph Cross
5 BS White Cross
Old Ralph Cross
418
4
429
Workings (dis)
Co Const
Workings (dis)
Rosedale Head
BS
Wether Hill
High Hill Top
BS
Spr
Workings (dis)
BS
Flat Howe
6
3
Grouse Butts
408
BSs
BSs
River Seven
Rosedale
Jackson's Road (Path)
Workings (disused)
Grouse Butts
410
South Flat Howe
Workings (disused)
400
2
390
Sprs
380
Workings (disused)
401
Gill Wath
Blakey Howe or Cockpit Hill
Blakey Swang
Waterfalls
BS
Spr
High Blakey Moor
The Lion Inn
Grouse Butts
Rain Gauge
Round Crag
Workings (disused)
1
Little Blakey Howe
BS
Grouse Butts
Quarry (dis)
Sheepfold
Quarry (dis)
Panniermans Spring
START
374
Sprs
Spr
Pile of Stones
346

▶ From the parking area at Little Blakey (where there is an open access information board), head north-west along the line of the dismantled railway. Follow the railway line as it curves with the valley, to the apex of its second bend and a plaque set into a stone ❶. The plaque is in memory of Ken Briggs 'who, as a cyclist, established this route as a bridleway'.

■ This is the Farndale branch of the railway line which served the iron-ore industry in Rosedale (see page 31). It has been used by walkers and cyclists for decades, but was only recently designated a bridleway. In the industrial heyday of the nineteenth century, trains chugged slowly around the head of this beautiful valley to Ingleby Incline, where the ore-laden wagons dropped steeply towards the railway trunk lines and civilization.

▶ Turn right on to High Blakey Moor. Jackson's Road is optimistically marked on the map, but there is no path on the ground. Initially there is a faint vehicle track, but when this disappears strike across the heather on the same trajectory, to the highest point. From here, continue to the next high point. The moor is generally dry and following the patches of burned or new-growth heather offers the line of least resistance. When the moor starts to drop away into Westerdale, bear right ❷. Look for a slender finger of stone on the horizon to the north-east and work towards it across the heather.

■ Westerdale is an isolated valley on the north side of the moor's watershed. Yorkshire's only salmon river, the Esk, rises here and the village of Westerdale is the first settlement on its banks. Hunters Sty Bridge, a centuries-old packhorse bridge, and a Victorian shooting lodge that now operates as a youth hostel, are the village's main points of interest.

Young Ralph's Cross in winter

▶ From the standing stone ❸, look north across the heather to locate a tall stone cross. Aim for a high point to its west (left). Soon a smaller stone cross will form a perfect silhouette against the skyline.

■ This is Old Ralph's Cross, at the high point where the moor drops into Westerdale, Esklets and Rosedale. The view is immense, across Danby Dale to the sea. A cross in this area is mentioned in the *Guisborough Charters* of 1200, and stories abound as to its origins and those of its neighbour, Young Ralph (see page 44 for the different legends associated with the crosses on the moors). One relates that Old Ralph is named after a dalesman who worked with the nuns of Rosedale Priory and lived to a great age.

▶ From Old Ralph's Cross ❹, bear due east for a short distance to Young Ralph's Cross, which you will find standing beside the road.

■ The original Young Ralph is also said to date from 1200. The current cross was probably erected in the eighteenth century and has been the symbol of the North York Moors National Park since 1974. One story tells that the cross was put up on the exact spot where a Danby farmer, named Ralph, found the body of a penniless traveller who had died from exhaustion. It is traditional to leave coins in a hard-to-reach scoop on the very top of the cross, to save other travellers from the same fate.

▶ Cross the road and strike over the moor to White Cross. If you need a break from untracked moorland, turn right and then left along the unclassified road.

■ Known locally as Fat Betty, White Cross stands on a pannier trod (see page 96) at the junction of Rosedale, Westerdale and Danby parishes. The cross is an ancient wheelhead set into a large stone plinth and is one of only two known wheelheads on these moors.

Three stories circulate regarding Betty's origins. One says that she takes her name from a nun at the Rosedale Priory. The nuns were known as the White Ladies because of their gowns of undyed wool. Another holds that Fat Betty was a woman who fell from her husband's horse and cart on a dark night. When he retraced his steps to find her, all that remained was this large stone. A third version (recounted in more detail on page 45) concerns the Old Ralph of Rosedale mentioned above. He rescued Sister Betty, Prioress of Rosedale, after she had become lost on the moors in a dense fog, finding her by the cross that now bears her name.

▸ At White Cross ❺, a signpost marking the Esk Valley Walk points north into Danby Dale and south towards Rosedale. Cross the road on the line of the south marker, back on to untracked moor.

■ The Esk Valley Walk, with its emblem of a leaping salmon, traces the River Esk from its source in Westerdale to the coast at Whitby. It starts at Castleton and loops up around Westerdale to this point on Danby Moor, before dropping down to Danby Dale and east along the river to the sea. The walk is 35 miles (56.5 km) long and includes some of North Yorkshire's most varied terrain.

▸ Walk straight down the moor towards the Rosedale branch of the dismantled railway line. The easiest route is to keep a line of grouse butts on your left and a deep stream cleft on your right. At the railway line, turn right ❻.

■ The whole of Rosedale stretches before you. Most of the line of the old railway is visible, sweeping around the head of the valley. To your right is the point where the line joined the Farndale branch for its run westward. To your left the line extends back to a series of dark arches, etched into the hillside. This is the branch opened in 1865 to serve the East Mines and their kilns; the arches are part of an extensive (and expensive) reconstruction carried out in the 1990s.

▶ Follow the railway line as it climbs slightly, past a brick ruin with an arched window. This is the remains of a water tank fed by leats (channels) from a small reservoir. A little further on is a signpost to the right, showing the way to the Lion Inn at Blakey.

■ The Lion Inn would come high on a list of Britain's most remote pubs. A hostelry since the sixteenth century, it stands at 1318 ft (402 m), almost the highest point of the North York Moors. The site is notorious for bad weather: the low-beamed bar is full of photographs showing the pub marooned in winter, and as recently as March 2005 it was cut off for days after snow drifted 14 ft (over 4 m) deep. Tales abound of locals heading there when storms are forecast, hoping for a legendary Lion Inn lock-in.

The pub has a long tradition of hospitality to walkers and the Coast to Coast and Lyke Wake Walks pass its door. It is also famed for its live music nights, when a stage is erected on the moor edge and bands play long and loud, with no fear of disturbing neighbours. Behind the inn is Blakey Howe, a neolithic burial mound, also known as Cockpit Hill after the cockfights that used to be staged there.

▶ If you aren't stopping for refreshment, continue along the railway line to a barrier warning off motorcycles and vehicles. Shortly after the barrier turn right up a small cutting, back to the starting point.

Iron awe

Rosedale, a deep valley in the heart of the North York Moors, is a magnet for all sorts of visitors. Walkers are drawn here by the footpaths and moorland, geologists visit for the subterranean delights of the Jurassic era and train enthusiasts come for the hiss of steam and the grind of couplings.

Actually, that last one's not true. They would have, though, if they'd lived a century and a half earlier. Why so confident? Because Rosedale's magnetism is due, in great part, to its iron industry and the railways that were created to service it.

Rosedale iron has been in use for at least 600 years, with bloomeries, or small furnaces, dotted around the valley from the fourteenth century. But this early flush of industry, along with the glass making of the sixteenth and seventeenth centuries, was small fry in comparison with the initiatives of the prosperous era to come.

The modern industrial age dawned in this dale in the 1850s, with open-cast quarrying on the west side of the valley. The new developments were to shape Rosedale and the lives of its citizens for the next seventy years.

In the early years of the industry, ore was taken by horse-drawn wagons to Pickering and then on by rail. This 'road' section was a trial, as a letter published in the *Malton Messenger* in February 1856 shows: 'The road from Cropton to Hartoft Bridge is a complete bog from end to end, full of clay holes, many two feet deep. . . . I noticed a waggon laden with iron ore, no less than eight horses yoked to it to drag it through the mire. The road to Rosedale is even worse.' But demand was high and despite the difficulties 4000 tons of ore were taken to Pickering in the first five years of extraction.

Something had to be done. A route for the railway was surveyed and, for reasons unclear to the general population, who thought it should run down the valley in the direction of Pickering, the line was laid over the high moors. It included two inclines: one at Rosedale at the east end of the track and the other above Ingleby at the west end.

The North Eastern Railway completed the Rosedale branch in 1861, the line travelling up the west side of the valley, around the head and back down the east side. But the mines were at the bottom of the dale and the railway line halfway up its sides. As a result, the ore had to be sent in rope-hauled wagons up nearly 400 vertical feet (120 metres) to the line at Bank Top. It was a dangerous, laborious process. In 1861 it was reported that 'a large number of waggons were being drawn up the incline when a coupling chain broke and the whole lot were seen rushing downwards with fearful rapidity, illuminating the line with fire, which in the darkness was truly awful.'

Probably the biggest enemy of the line was the weather. Winters on the high moors are severe and snow was a seasonal problem, especially on the exposed lands around Blakey. In 1882 the line was completely blocked by a single snowstorm in early December; the snow lay until February.

Despite these harsh conditions, industry thrived. The population of this quiet valley soared, peaking at almost 3000 in the 1870s. Rows of cottages were built around the fringes of the dale for the miners, although Rosedale Abbey remained the only village.

Over sixty-five years, the line carried 10 million tons of ironstone. It was closed in 1929 after the mines were abandoned. But this piece of history hasn't entirely disappeared: while the railway tracks and mines are long gone, relics of the infrastructure remain and are part of the heart of the moors.

The bed of the railway has long been used as a track for walking and cycling. Bank Top, above

Rosedale on the west side, at the top of what is locally known as Chimney Bank, is the access point for most visitors to the line.

The railway was also responsible for the immense engine house chimney, which became a prominent local landmark. Known as Rosedale Chimney, it stood for 112 years at the top of the bank before being demolished in 1972. It was constructed by John Flintoft of Lastingham, who is said to have danced on the top when he finished the job. The chimney was much taller than was necessary because the landowner didn't want its smoke to upset his grouse.

A row of cottages, built for railway workers at Bank Top, still stand and, while less isolated than in earlier times, continue to rely on generators for power.

Old ironstone workings, Rosedale

Further along the railway, on the first major bend as the line sweeps around the valley, is Sheriff's Pit. A tottering ruin marks the deep shaft sunk to the iron source, 260 feet (80 metres) below. The idea was to save money by hauling ore up the shaft, rather than using the expensive and dangerous incline. However, the shaft became waterlogged and local youngsters had to be employed to pump and bail water from the pit. The gear was removed from Sheriff's Pit in 1911. Today the open shaft, fenced off but still visible, along with the rubble of the manager's house and the workshops, are the most obvious remains.

Blakey Junction, where the line eased out of Rosedale and into Farndale, is near the head of the valley on the west side. After making its way in a great loop around Farndale, the line ran via Blowath Crossing to Ingleby Incline, the western equivalent of Rosedale's Bank Top. With a maximum gradient of 1 in 5, this mile-long (1.6-kilometre) incline was an accident blackspot. The ore's journey took just three minutes at twenty miles per hour; runaway wagons were common.

On the east side of Rosedale is the best-preserved remnant of the valley's railway and iron industry. The East Mines calcinating kilns, into which the ore was tipped to be heated, have been restored and provide the focus of a railway walk. Graceful arches of soft sandstone soar above the old line and offer a whisper of this dale's recent history.

The kilns give a fine vantage point over Rosedale. A patchwork quilt of green fields rises to the rough and tumble of heather moorland, the old railway line forming a neat seam between the two. You may hear the cur-lee of a curlew or the pee-wit of a lapwing – and if you listen really carefully, if you strain your ears at the wind, you may just hear the hiss and shooop of a long-gone steam train, labouring around the valley.

WALK 2

SPAUNTON ESTATE

DIFFICULTY 👢👢👢 **DISTANCE 8¾ miles (14 km)**

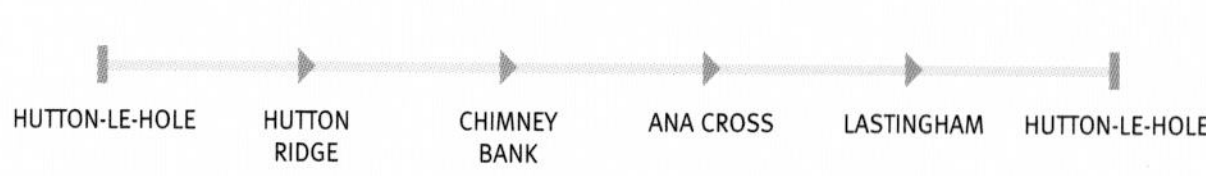

MAP OS Explorer OL26, North York Moors (Western Area)

STARTING POINT Hutton-le-Hole (GR 705900)

PUBLIC TRANSPORT Moorsbus services M1, M3, M5 and M53 (see page 77) serve Hutton-le-Hole. Local bus services 174 and 176 also run from Pickering and Kirkbymoorside, May–September (call W.P. Hutchinson on 01347 821853).

PARKING In the public car park in Hutton-le-Hole

A walk crossing high heather uplands, with an insight into early Christianity on the moors. There are options to avoid the rougher terrain.

▸ If you arrived by Moorsbus, begin this walk at the drop-off point, the Ryedale Folk Museum. With the museum in front of you, turn left up the village street and right up a narrow road, signed to the public car park.

■ Hutton-le-Hole is one of North Yorkshire's most charming, and most visited, villages. Stone houses are dotted around a village green where sheep graze freely. Hutton Beck, a favourite spot for picnickers, flows through the green in a lazy serpentine. Once a stronghold of the weaving industry, today the village's main claim to fame is the Ryedale Folk Museum.

An acclaimed open-air museum set in 2½ acres, it recreates North Yorkshire life over a 4000-year period. Visitors can wander through historic buildings such as the oldest photographic studio in Britain, complete with its equipment, and an Elizabethan manor house with massive oak crucks. Thatched cottages from the eighteenth and nineteenth centuries, which have been relocated here from Harome and Danby, contain treasures such as salt boxes and witch posts (see page 152). There are also workshops that would have been used by traditional craftsmen such as cobblers, coopers, tinsmiths and wheelwrights. Craft demonstrations, rare-breed displays and historic re-enactments are frequent throughout the summer.

▶ From the car park, continue up the hill and, when the road curves right, bear left and head through a gate on to the moors ❶. Two green tracks are visible. Take the right track which climbs slightly, then follows the curve of moorland around and up towards the low ridge.

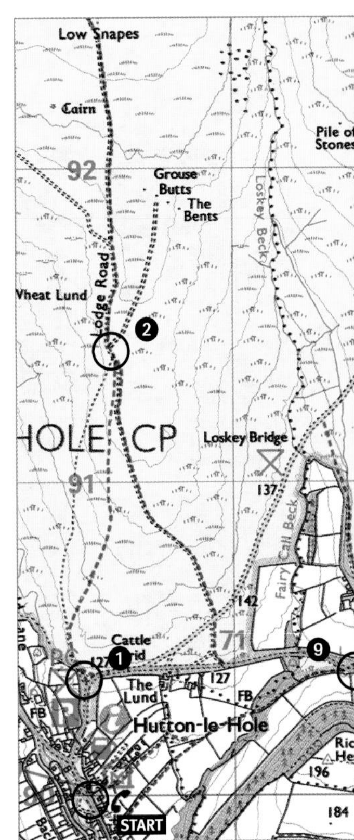

■ You are walking through the Manor of Spaunton, which includes the villages of Lastingham, Spaunton, Appleton-le-Moors, Rosedale West and Hutton-le-Hole (the 'le', incidentally, has no French link but is a Victorian affectation, most likely an invention of the Post Office). By the time of the Norman Conquest, Spaunton Manor was substantial and belonged to Gamel, owner of great estates throughout England. After the Conquest,

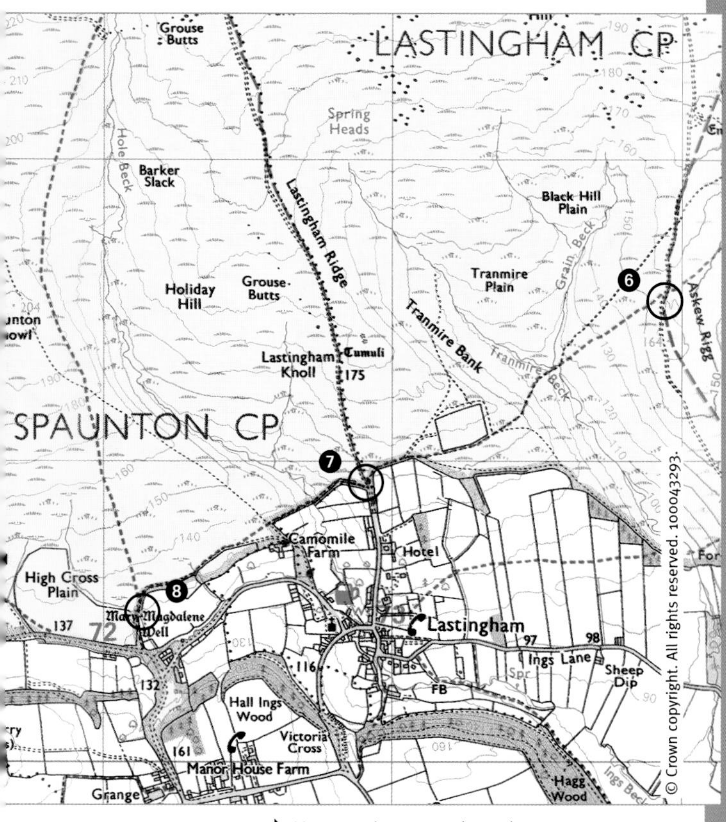

▶ Map continues northwards on pages 38–9

the manor was given to St Mary's Abbey in York and its holdings were increased by gifts of land from other estates in the area.

After the Dissolution of the Monasteries in the 1530s, the estate became the property of Sir John Bulmer of Riseborough and then of Lord Grey de Wilton, whose successors sold off chunks of land to freeholders. The Darley family bought the Manor of Spaunton in 1780. The current lord of the manor, George

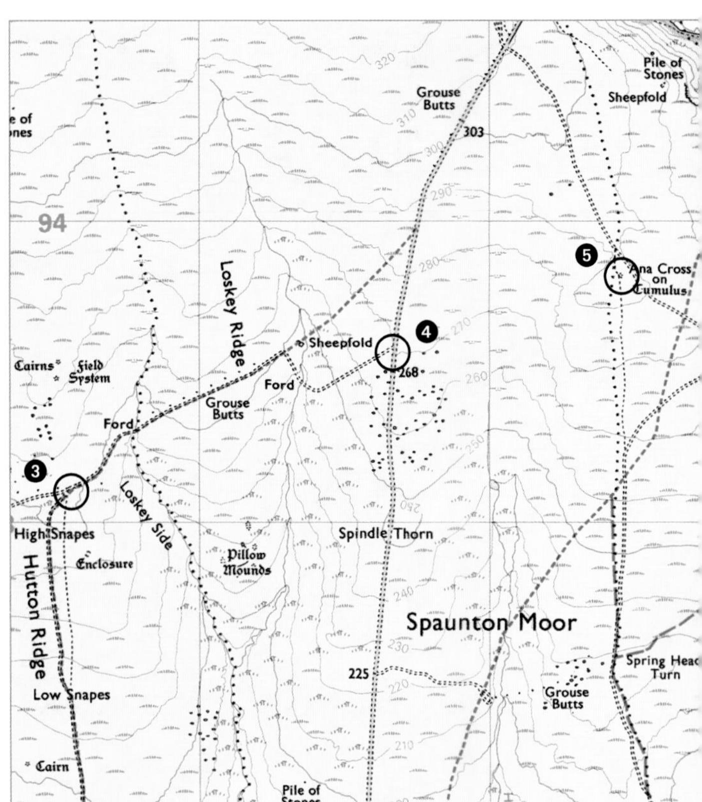

Winn-Darley, runs the 7000-acre estate from Barmoors, a large house visible across the valley on your left. For 200 years the land has been used mainly for grouse shooting, which, along with the farming of 5000 sheep, is the mainstay of the estate's commercial activities.

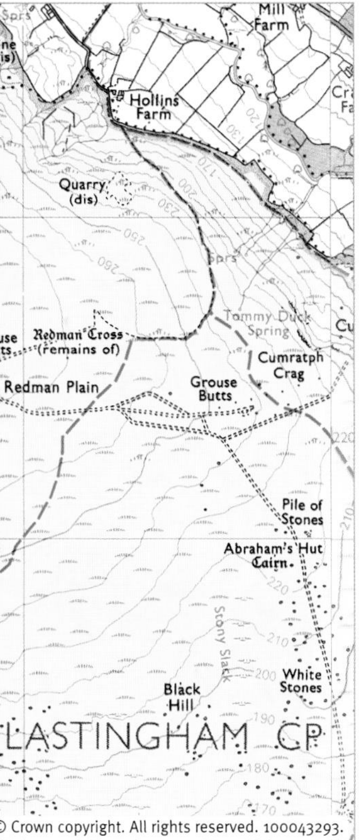

▶ A stone block marks the point where this track meets the access road to Spaunton Lodge ❷. Cross the road and pick up a faint track across the moor (an easier option is to take the footpath marked on the OS map to point ❸). Follow the curve of the moor left, until you are walking north. Pass between two wooden grouse butts (these are contemporary; traditional butts are half circles of stone and earth). You should be walking in the general direction of a lump on the skyline, which is a tumulus or burial mound.

■ Iron Age tumuli, or 'howes' as they were called by later Norse settlers, once dotted the horizon in all directions. Today they remain conspicuous features on the high moors, the three howes near Bank Top being among the largest. The elevated positions of the howes were probably chosen to allow local chiefs, in their last resting place, to look over the lands they had ruled in their lifetime.

▶ The track soon disappears. At this point Loskey Beck, the stream in the valley to your right, divides. Aim for the head of the left (west) fork, walking through untracked heather and bilberry. Soon you will see a deep trench with banks either side, and a line of wooden grouse butts. Follow the line up the hill; depending on the time of year there may be a path mown between them.

At the end of the line, aim right towards a tall post and join a vehicle track ❸. Turn right. You can now see your next target, Ana Cross, on the skyline. Follow the broad track down hill and up the moor to a tarmac road ❹.

If conditions are dry, you can cross the road and walk straight to Ana Cross but there is no path and the central area of this section is a bog. Otherwise, turn left up the road for 500 yards (500 m) until you reach an unofficial car parking area at the top of Chimney Bank, above Rosedale. Turn right on to the well-used track to the cross ❺.

■ Ana Cross (according to the Ordnance Survey map) or Ainhowe Cross (according to local lore) is a prominent landmark on Spaunton Moor. She is nearly 10 ft (3 m) tall, made of sandstone and scored with iron ore. Her perch is a tumulus on a branch of the ancient path from Farndale to Rosedale known as the Beggar's Track, and she is visible for miles.

Like many moorland crosses, Ana has had an eventful past, having toppled over on several occasions. The man who put her back on her feet most recently, in the mid-1990s, was Geoff Dring, a stonemason and farmer in nearby Hartoft valley. In a labour of love, he hauled the stone column from his land, carved it by hand and erected the new cross on the moor. From its plinth, the view is immense: east across the farmland of Rosedale to the gloom of Cropton Forest, south and west to the lower plains and escarpments towards Malton and Bilsdale, and north over unbroken heather moorland. (See page 46 for more about Ana Cross.)

▶ From the cross, take a small path heading due east. After 20 yards (20 m) this joins a shooting track; turn right and follow it down the moor. At a crossroads continue straight on, staying on the main track as it rolls down the moor.

As the track starts to rise after a prolonged descent, look for a sandstone cairn on the right ❻. This marks a footpath crossing the track on a diagonal, although if the heather is in bloom it may be difficult to see. Turn right and follow this path down the hill and across Tranmire Beck. Climb the steep bank on the far side of the stream and take the track to the top of the ridge. Continue straight on to a stone wall and follow it to the Lastingham Millennium Stone, at a track junction ❼.

■ From this junction, it is worth dropping into the pretty village of Lastingham, where you will find the imposing church of St Mary's and its ancient crypt. A monastery was founded here in 654 by Cedd, Bishop of the East Saxons (see page 66). It was nearly destroyed by Viking and Danish invaders, and by 1078, when the monk Stephen arrived from Whitby and began his restoration, the monastery was unoccupied. Today the site is an atmospheric place, evoking whispers of ageless Christianity, and it is easily visited from inside the church.

If it's time for a break, the Blacksmith's Arms opposite the church welcomes walkers.

▶ Once refreshed, retrace your steps to the Millennium Stone on the moor. Take the footpath that heads downhill in the direction of High Cross. Stay close to the wall across Hole Beck and up the other side. When the path curves left by a stand of larch, bear right on to the moor ❽, heading for a group of trees.

■ The early inhabitants of Lastingham worshipped the water nymphs, to whom they believed they owed the sweet water which flowed in their springs. When the monks arrived in Lastingham in the seventh century the

wells were reconsecrated to Christian saints, including St Chad, St Cedd and St Mary Magdalene. Here the main footpath passes close to the Well of Mary Magdalene, a stone trough positioned under a small spring.

▶ At the trees turn right and follow the fence as it loops around High Cross Plain.

Ancient signpost near Hutton-le-Hole

Cross the ditch, the access road to Bainwood Head and a small piece of moor to arrive at a tarmac road. Turn right and, after about 100 yards (100 m), turn left up a raised footpath ⑨. Follow the footpath through woods and over fields back into Hutton-le-Hole. Turn right on to the village street and return to the start. Alternatively, from Bainwood follow the road back to the car park.

Moorland crosses

On the edge of a small moorland village are two stone crosses. They look more like lumps, but they're crosses all the same. Word is that they point the way to ancient farmsteads, including Hamley where a ghost walks the lane . . .

The village is Appleton-le-Moors, a medieval settlement whose name has changed with the centuries. But the names of the crosses haven't changed: High Cross and Low Cross have always been so. And the moors are riddled with their siblings, which come in all shapes and sizes and often don't even look like crosses. Besides the classic shaft and crosshead arrangement, there are wheelhead crosses, crosses that look like a pestle and mortar and crosses that are simply rounded pillars pierced with a hole.

For years, walkers have rested on their plinths, used them for taking compass bearings in the mist and felt along their upper arms for money (if you find a coin on a cross you take it; if there's no coin there, you leave one). There are more standing stones and wayside crosses here than anywhere else in the country. More than a thousand have been erected over the centuries, but only around forty of them have been given names.

The most famous cross is Young Ralph's Cross (Walk 1), used as an emblem by the North York Moors National Park. It's also the most spectacular, standing tall on the roadside on Blakey Ridge. This is the geographic centre of the North York Moors, and the junction of a number of ancient ridgeways. Right on the top of Young Ralph's Cross is a hollow for hiding coins, but you need incredibly long arms, or a horse, or a hoist on someone's back to reach into it.

Young Ralph has an elderly companion, Old Ralph, a few long strides to the west. Perched high on a ridgeway dividing Esklets, Westerdale and Rosedale, Old Ralph has a fantastic view over the moors to the sea. It's an atmospheric place: dark pools of water separate the blonde reeds at his base and wind tugs at the heather. A cross called Crucem Radulphi, possibly named after Bishop Ralph of Guisborough Priory, is mentioned in the *Guisborough Charters* of 1200, so Old Ralph really is the old man of the moors. But Young Ralph isn't young at all: it is likely that the original cross here also dated back to 1200, and there are records from 1550 showing that it was, at that time, made of wood.

About twenty minutes' walk over the moor from these two gents is Fat Betty, a sturdy base topped by a wheelhead cross. To create a wheelhead the top of the stone is widened into a roughly circular shape and pierced four times to make a cross. Fat Betty is also called White Cross and she is indeed painted white. She has a wonderful view down the valley of Rosedale, and marks the junction of the parishes of Danby, Westerdale and Rosedale.

Tall tales abound about this trio of crosses. Local people used to say that the world would end when three kings met at Ralph Cross, although the current lack of kings in waterproof boots probably means we're safe in the short term.

The best-known story is that Old Ralph was 'Aud Ralph Roas'le' (Old Ralph of Rosedale), a local man who was hired to accompany the prioresses of Rosedale and Baysdale abbeys on a tour of the moors to resolve a boundary dispute. When the women became lost in a dense fog, Old Ralph began to search the moors for them. Luckily, he found Sister Betty by the cross that now bears her name and Sister Margery by a large upright stone, now known as Margery Stone, which marks the junction of the Lyke Wake Walk and Blakey Ridge. In reality, Margery Stone is a boundary stone of the Feversham estate – but why should facts spoil a good story? The end of the tale is that Old Ralph, being a gentleman, reunited the women where his cross now stands.

Near Fat Betty is Botton Cross. It's now just a shaft with three 'ears' sticking out of a medieval stone base; monastic records from 1234 refer to it as Bothine Cross. The treat here, on the flanks of Danby Moor, is the view rather than the relic, across the northern moors to the sea.

Swivelling around to face south and walking along the disused railway line for about 7 miles (12 kilometres) brings you to Ana Cross (Walk 2). (It's marked as Ana on the Ordnance Survey map, but local opinion comes down in favour of Ainhowe.)

Ana is a golden goddess, made of local sandstone. Her name refers to the name of the original Anglo-Saxon cross, the head of which lies in the eleventh-century crypt of St Mary's church in the nearby village of Lastingham. The original cross was more than twenty-three feet (seven metres) high, making it the largest known pre-Norman monument in England.

Over to the east is another clutch of crosses. At their heart is Lilla, the oldest Christian monument in the north of England. Reached by a boot-sucking hike up Fylingdales Moor, Lilla stands on a grassy burial mound with a clear view over heather to the wild east coast.

This cross is supposed to mark the grave of Lilla, chief minister to King Edwin of Deira. In 626 he saved the life of the King when he flung himself between Edwin and an assailant's poisoned, two-edged dagger. It's unlikely, however, that Lilla is buried in the howe, or mound, because excavations around it in the 1920s revealed pieces of jewellery dated between 200 and 500 years later than Lilla's death.

Lilla Cross is an unusual shape, with a squat cross-head perched on a tall, chunky shaft. The letter G for Goathland is carved on the north-west face; on the opposite side is a C for Chomley estate, and a cross.

About 3 miles (5 kilometres) to the south-west, at the foot of Whinny Nab, is Malo Cross (Walk 12). The initials R, E and K, which are carved on its east face, are explained in records of the Duchy of Lancaster dated 1619. 'Richard Egerton, Knight', is accused by the Duchy, who owned the land, of 'trespass and encroachment for setting up a boundary stone with a cross'.

This ancient dispute is further proof that moorland crosses were erected for a variety of reasons. Some were set up to mark the boundaries of monastic sheep-grazing land. Others were preaching crosses, places where itinerant monks would bring the gospel to pagan communities. In the Middle Ages crosses were also put up as waymarks to guide travellers over the featureless expanses of the moors. The crosses helped to mark routes, which often turned into roads as they carried increasing amounts of traffic.

Many crosses have a scoop on the top where passers-by traditionally place coins for more needy travellers. A rhyme about the now-vanished Cropton Cross suggests that more immediate succour may have sometimes been at hand:

On Cropton Cross there is a cup
And in that cup there is a sup
Take that cup and drink that sup
And put the cup back on the cross top.

View down Farndale

WALK 3

BRANSDALE MOOR

DIFFICULTY **DISTANCE 8¾ miles (14 km)**

MAP OS Explorer OL26, North York Moors (Western Area)

STARTING POINT Bransdale (GR 613975)

PUBLIC TRANSPORT There is no public transport into Bransdale. The nearest access point is Church Houses in Farndale, which can be reached by Moorsbus M53 (see page 77). This would add an extra 6¼ miles (10 km) to the route, walking via Monket Bank and Rudland Rigg to Cockan Cross.

PARKING On the roadside. Please take care not to obstruct this narrow, gated road.

A walk across a wild, windswept moor, with glimpses of historic religion and railways. The route is mainly on shooting tracks, finishing on footpaths across farmland.

▶ A narrow, gated road accesses Cockayne, a clutch of farmhouses at the head of Bransdale. Park on the grass verge on the west side of the valley; there is room for two cars before the gate, beside a footpath and bridleway junction. Walk up the moor side. The easiest route is on the footpath but the moor here is thick with bilberry, which is less arduous to walk over than the taller, denser heather. Near the top of the moor, regardless of where you make the ascent, you will meet a track. If you are on the footpath, you will end the climb facing Stump Cross ❶.

■ Stump Cross is a fat knuckle of sandstone nested in a socket on a large sandstone base. In common with many of the moorland crosses in this area, the arrangement strongly resembles a pestle and mortar. The shaft is broken but it is thought that the original cross had a carved, outstretched hand. This belief is supported by records from 1829 which call it 'the cross with the hand'.

▶ Turn right and follow this track – an ancient road known as Thurkilsti – around the head of the valley. (Thurkilsti is also visited in Walk 6). Just before it crosses Hodge Beck, which splits the dale, the track passes a group of pancaked, sandstone rocks which make an excellent place for a picnic ❷.

■ Hodge Beck, which rises just north of this point, rushes directly down Bransdale, before joining the River Dove and then the River Rye on its journey to the sea. On the way it passes the beautiful church of St Gregory's Minster at Kirkdale, which is world-famous for its Saxon sundial (see page 67).

▶ Stay on the track to cross Hodge Beck and then turn left at a junction. Follow this to a T-junction at Cockayne Head and turn right ❸. Pass a stone waymark and a stone grouse butt and, as the track begins to descend, turn left across the moor ❹. The easiest way is on a faint grass track which descends to meet a wide track. Turn left and continue until the track appears to disappear into thin air ❺.

■ This is the top of Ingleby Incline, a crucial component of the railway line built in the nineteenth century to transport iron ore from Rosedale, two valleys away.

The incline's gradient of 1 in 5 was lethal for heavily loaded wagons and accidents were common (see page 34). Today the slope is marked by immense beams of wood scored with rusting metal rods, vast stone blocks and the remains of winding gear.

The view ahead is striking, along the rugged western escarpment of the North York Moors. At the end of the scarp is the hooked profile of Roseberry Topping, at 1056 ft (322 m) the Matterhorn of the moors. The shape isn't natural: the mountain was so heavily mined and quarried for alum, iron ore, jet and roadstone that a chunk eventually fell away, wreaking havoc in the villages below. The hill and its surrounding moorland are riddled with footpaths, offering pleasant walking with far-reaching views.

▶ Turn sharply right and walk across the moor to reach a wide track. Turn right and start the long hike along the ridge.

■ This is the ancient Rudland Rigg road, which crosses one of the largest stretches of uninhabited moorland in North Yorkshire. It has

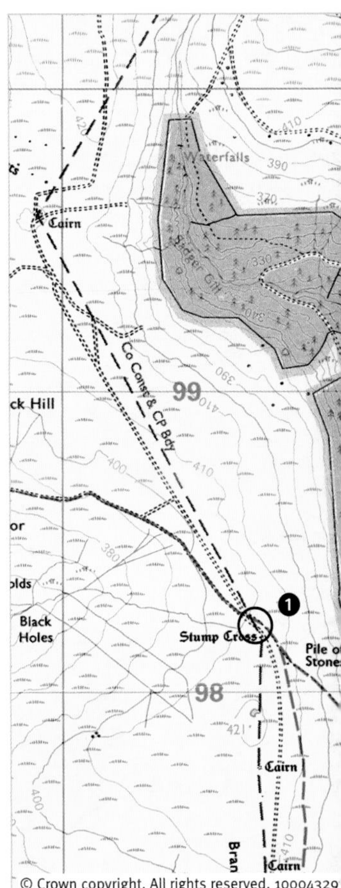

probably been in use for more than 2000 years. Much more recent, but in keeping with the bleak, timeless feel of the moor, is the tall stone marker that soon looms on your right. Marked 'Sir W Fowells' on the north face and '1888' on the south, it is most likely a boundary stone.

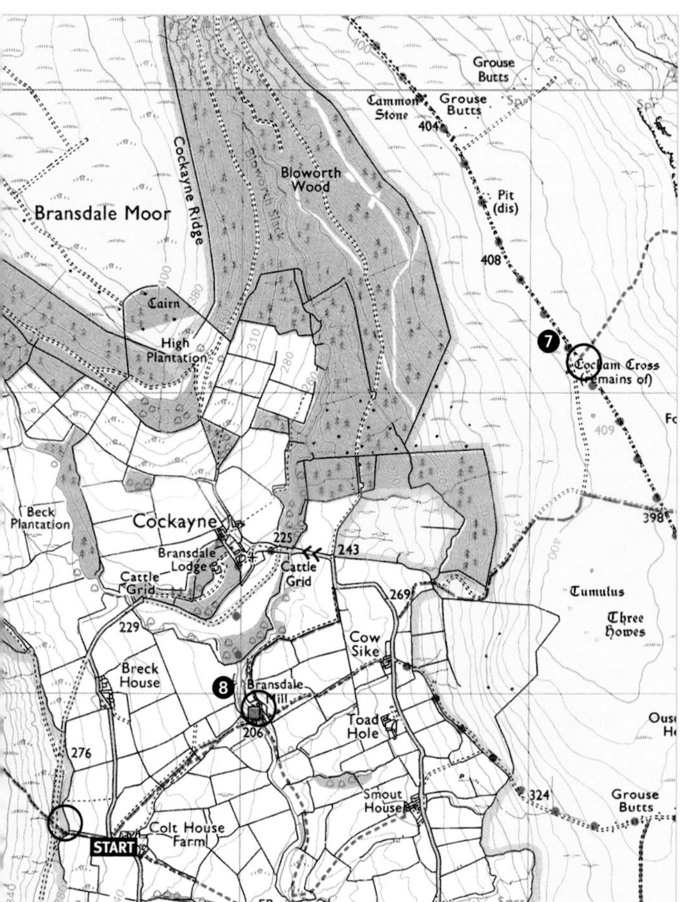

▶ Map continues northwards on pages 54–5

Beside it is the remains of a small stone cross, which has a notch in the top for coins (see page 47).

▶ Continue along the track as it crosses the line of the old railway at Bloworth Crossing ❻. Follow the track as it dips and climbs for 2 miles (3 km) to a small post with a footpath marker, on your left. Turn right and walk across the moor towards a stone shaft, which is the remains of Cockan Cross ❼.

■ Cockan Cross overlooks the valley of Bransdale. All that can be seen today is a broken shaft in a medieval base, with another piece of broken stone, possibly also part of the shaft, beside it. The cross is carved on four sides, to be used as a waymark. Directions to Bransdale and Farndale are still decipherable, with the lettering for Kirby (for Kirkbymoorside) and Stoxl (for Stokesley) already fading to a blur.

▶ Turn left at the cross and continue over the moor until you meet a faint grassy track. Turn right. This path soon becomes a rough track that curves around

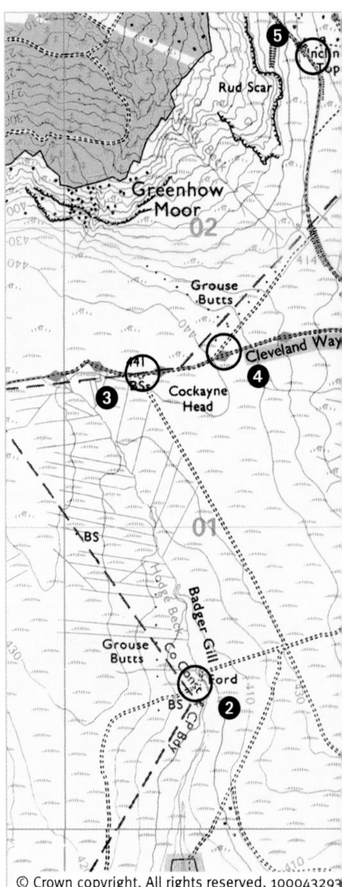

the hill and down into farmland (now as a sunken track). Follow the track through a gate in a high dry-stone wall and across a field to the road.

■ There is a lovely view from here to imposing Bransdale Lodge and the tiny church of St Nicholas. A chapel of

▶ page 58

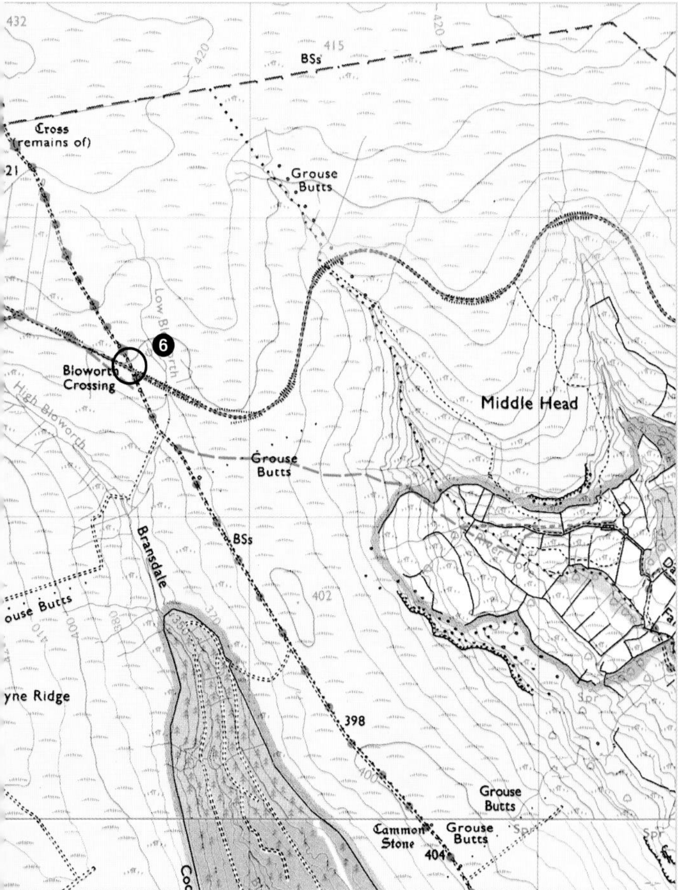

Roseberry Topping

ease was built here after the Norman Conquest, but this small stone building dates from 1886. It is delightful inside and out, with carved wooden pews, a barrel roof, a nave, a small chancel, a tiny west tower with two bells and an ancient Norman font in the churchyard. Electricity was installed in 2004. Services take place on the first Sunday of every month and legendary teas are served on some Saturdays and Bank Holiday Mondays from May until September.

▶ Turn left on to the road and almost immediately right, following footpath waymarks. Follow the waymarks across a series of fields, and down a steep flight of carved stone steps into the bottom of the valley. Here Hodge Beck races through a complex of stone buildings, which form Bransdale Mill ❽.

■ Most of Bransdale is owned by the National Trust and this mill is no exception. Immaculately restored, the stone buildings show off superb stonework, all hand-feathered.

On the east side of the river, inside a building attached to the main house, is a large waterwheel in a surprisingly good state of repair. On the west side, across a bridge, is a small stone building which houses a large trough that is fed with fresh water by carved stone chutes. Ferns and mosses grow on the inside walls.

Further up the hill, with a grand view back to Bransdale Lodge, is a large sandstone sundial. The phrase 'Time and life move slowly' is carved on one face.

▶ From the mill, follow footpath markers up the hill, through fields to a road. Cross the road and climb up an old track between two stone walls, signposted as a bridleway, to the moorland road where you started.

WALK 4

ARDEN GREAT MOOR

DIFFICULTY 👢👢 **DISTANCE 9 miles (14.5 km)**

MAP OS Explorer OL26, North York Moors (Western Area)

STARTING POINT Roadside clearing at Square Corner, at the start of Hambleton Street (GR 479959)

PUBLIC TRANSPORT The Moorsbus M9 (see page 77) runs to Square Corner. Abbotts of Leeming run a year-round Northallerton–Stokesley service via Osmotherley (route 80/89); call 01677 422858 for more information.

PARKING In the clearing

A gentle walk around the edge of Arden Great Moor, with almost limitless views in all directions. There is one stage over rough heather; otherwise the walk is entirely on well-made tracks.

▸ From the parking area at Square Corner, above Osmotherley village, walk south on Hambleton Street, an ancient drove road that follows the western escarpment of the Hambleton Hills.

■ Hambleton Street was one of the most important drove tracks on the eighteenth-century run from Scotland

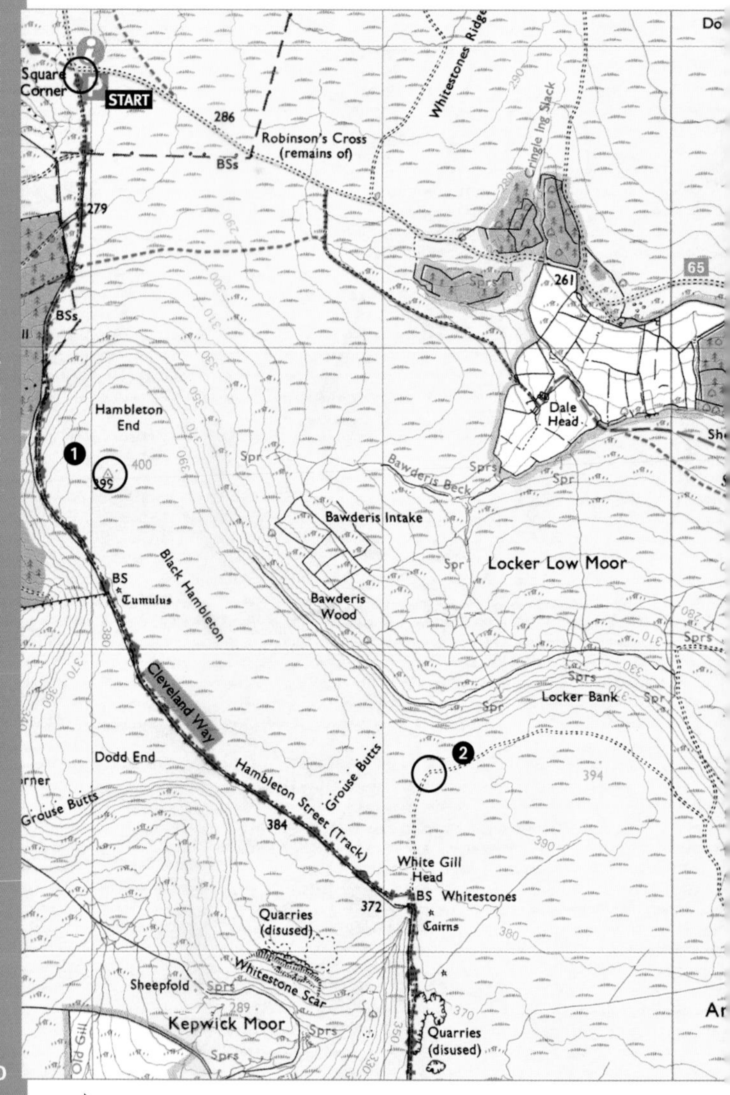

▶ Map continues southwards on pages 62–3

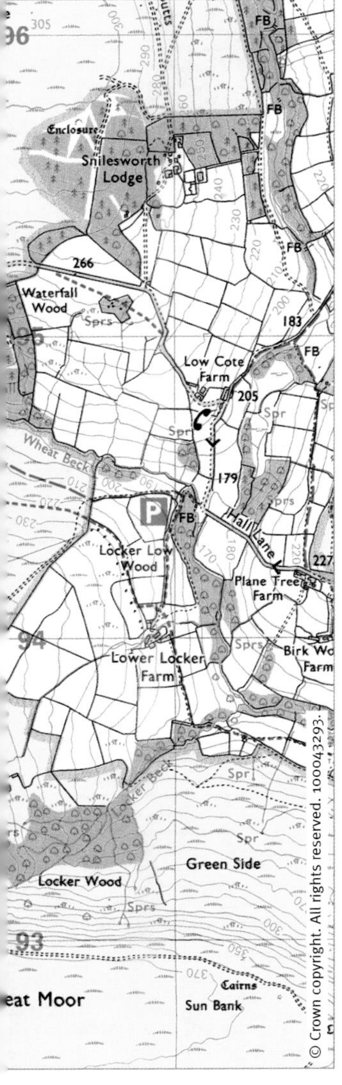

to the cattle markets in England. The path pre-dates the Romans, however, and there are numerous Bronze and Iron Age earthworks along its route.

Drovers keen to avoid expensive tolls and turnpikes stayed high on the moors, moving huge herds along this ancient route. From Durham cattle were taken east of the main toll road through Yarm to Swainby and then up on to the Cleveland Hills. The drove road ran south, keeping to the high, fairly level ground of the Hambleton Hills.

The cattle fared well on this route, with plenty of wide grass verges, particularly between Oldstead and Coxwold. And the drovers fared even better, with so many pubs that many arrived drunk at the road end, their dogs in sole control of the cattle. Inns along the way included Dialstone House and the Hambleton Hotel on Sutton Bank and the Scotch Corner Inn at Oldstead. Today the Hambleton, near the national park visitor centre

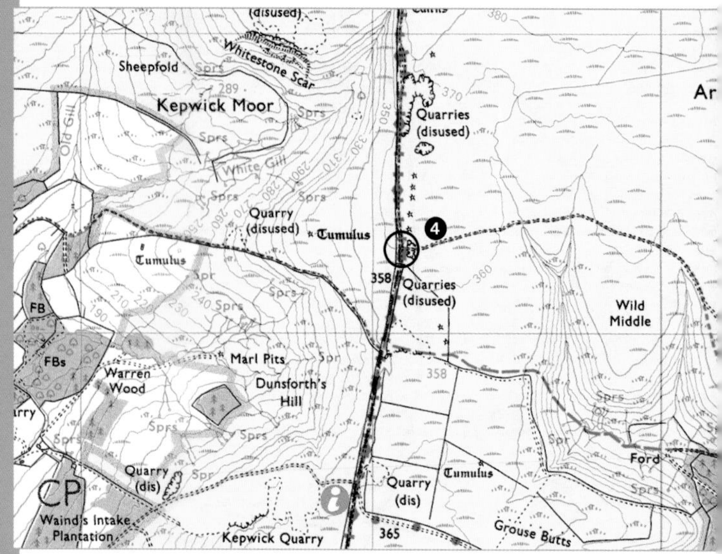

at Sutton Bank, is the only one still trading.

▶ Ahead is the large dome of Hambleton End. Climb to the trig point at 1309 ft (399 m) ❶. The easiest route is to continue up the drove road to a large stone cairn and turn left on to a small track, heading across the moor to the concrete marker. Then turn right and walk across the heather moor, keeping the escarpment close on your left, until you meet a rough estate track. Turn left ❷.

■ The view north and east over the Cleveland Hills is immense. A vast swathe of rough moorland split by steep cliffs and sharp-sided valleys stretches to the far horizon. Numerous rivers are born here and wells, including Grey Stone Well, Holy Well and Nuns' Well, dot the wet, spring-laden hills. In August these hills are ablaze with purple, but for much of the year they are brown, brooding and empty.

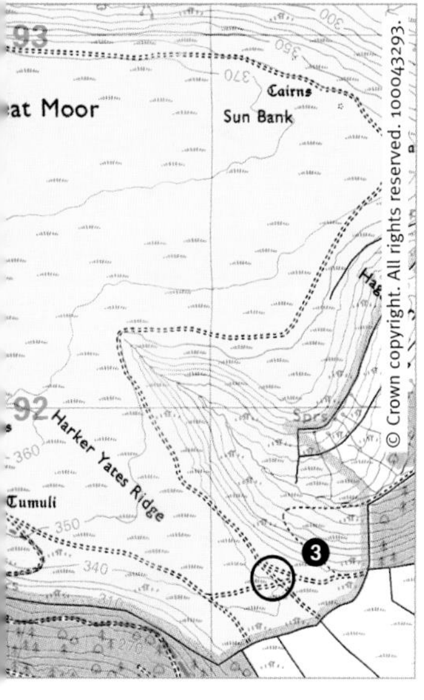

▶ The track winds around the edge of the Arden Great Moor plateau. A fence was erected across the western edge in 2005 and the track negotiates this via a large gate. Stay on the track as it passes around the deep cleft formed by the infant Eskerdale Beck. When the track divides, with paths towards North Moor and Arden Hall, bear right ❸.

■ Arden Hall is now below you, hidden in dense woodland. It was built on the site of a Benedictine nunnery, which became a seat of the Tancred family in 1564. The only portion of the convent buildings incorporated in the present mansion is an old chimney, which was probably in the nuns' kitchen. The classically proportioned frontage seen today was built in the seventeenth century.

At the time of the Domesday Book Arden belonged to the manor of Bagby. It then formed part of the lands of Hugh, son of Baldric, and subsequently came into the possession of the Hoton, or Hutton, family. Peter de Hoton founded a Benedictine nunnery here in about 1150, which he endowed with a gift of land and dedicated to St Andrew. At the Dissolution of the Monasteries, Henry VIII granted the nunnery and its possessions to Thomas Culpeper, and they later passed into the hands of the Tancreds.

In a little wood behind the hall is the Nuns' Well, from which a stream continues to flow. Near it, in 1885, a piece of stone cross 3 ft (1 m) long was unearthed, and in the same year a quantity of human bones were found beneath the floor of Arden Hall's laundry.

▶ The sloping moor to your right is known as Harker Yates Ridge. Follow the track along its north-west flank, past Wild Middle (the origins of this glorious name remain a mystery), back to Hambleton Street. Turn right ❹.

■ The Cleveland Way runs along Hambleton Street (which forms the western part of the walk). This long-distance path of 109 miles (176 km) runs from Helmsley, around the top of the North York Moors and down the coast to Filey. It offers a heady mix of coast and moorland, as well as glimpses of the area's industrial and cultural heritage.

The grand opening of the Cleveland Way took place in 1969, four years after the Pennine Way was opened. Since then it has been joined with the Wolds Way and the Ebor Way, with the missing link (the footpath signposted as the Link) created in 1975 to form a southern route that returns walkers to Helmsley.

▶ Enjoying the enormous views to the west, follow Hambleton Street back to the giant stone cairn at the foot of Black Hambleton and down the hill to the starting point.

■ The orange-tiled roofs of Osmotherley, and the small reservoir by Jenny Brewster's

Spring, are clearly visible on the left. Osmotherley is a picturesque little village with pretty stone-built cottages and a cross in the middle of a green. Next to the cross is a stone table where Methodist John Wesley once preached; near by is his Methodist chapel, built in 1754 and one of the oldest such chapels in the world.

Surrounded by moors and pastureland, the village has a long association with farming. The market place was used for sheep and cattle sales until quite recently. Smugglers were also known to frequent the village, as they crossed the moors with contraband from the coast. Today's visitors are mostly walkers and cyclists. Osmotherley is the starting point of the Lyke Wake Walk, covering 42 miles (68 km) of moorland to Ravenscar on the coast. The Cleveland Way also runs through the village and Wainwright's famous Coast to Coast Walk passes close by.

View west from Arden Great Moor

Seeds of faith

Small stone churches nestle into flower-filled valleys, ancient arches soar against a backdrop of woodland. Visitors to the North York Moors marvel at the ruined abbeys; local people worship at the sturdy moorland chapels.

Since the seventh century, when Christianity came to the moors via Whitby and Lastingham, religion has had a major hand in shaping this region and its people. While the early seeds of faith were trampled by Viking invaders, they soon reasserted themselves and by the end of the tenth century Christianity was widespread. Monks gained land, wealth and power, and held sway over much of the moors until Henry VIII's Dissolution of the Monasteries in the sixteenth century. The monks laid pathways, created farms, developed industries, and built priories and abbeys that can still be seen today. Probably the most famous, or at least most visited, religious centres are St Mary's in Lastingham (Walk 2) and Rievaulx Abbey, at the southern edge of the moor. But there are also other places that help tell the story.

A pioneer into what was then the dangerous back country of Northumbria, St Cedd started to build his monastery at Lastingham in 654. St Bede described the place as being 'among steep and solitary hills, where you would rather look for the hiding places of robbers or the lairs of wild animals than the abodes of man.' This was hardly a description of an ideal site for a religious house. St Cedd succumbed to illness just ten years later and was laid to rest in Lastingham.

His monastery was later sacked by the Vikings and in 1078, when the monk Stephen arrived from Whitby, it was unoccupied. Stephen's restoration included building a crypt with a nave and side aisles, which was unique in England at that time. Almost a decade after Stephen's arrival, he was driven out by robbers and outlaws and the monastery ceased to exist. By the thirteenth century it had become the parish church of St Mary's and today is the focal point of the tranquil village of Lastingham. Besides being used for conventional services, it hosts events such as candlelit concerts of classical music.

Rievaulx's origins are later, dating from the arrival of a Cistercian order of monks from France in 1131. The small community worked hard and flourished. By the time of St Aelred, the third abbot, there were around 150 ordained monks and 600 lay brethren. They were given rough land by a local landowner and managed to graze huge flocks of sheep; the wool produced was sought after throughout Europe. The monks also developed ironstone mining and cleared forests to provide fuel for the furnaces. To transport their produce, they built roads, bridges and canals. And of course they built Rievaulx Abbey itself, an architectural wonder, a symphony in stone.

Other churches, less august but equally evocative, include St Gregory's Minster in Kirkdale, near the market town of Kirkbymoorside. A beautiful example of a pre-Norman church, it has an idyllic woodland setting and in spring is surrounded by daffodils and bluebells. Its main claim to fame, apart from its glorious location, is its unique Saxon sundial. This is embedded in the wall over what is now the main door to the church, under the porch roof that protects the entrance.

An inscription on the sundial in Old English states that the church was completely rebuilt in the middle of the eleventh century at the initiative of a Scandinavian man named 'Orm, son of Gamal'. Considerable parts of Orm's reconstruction remain, although the building has been substantially altered over succeeding centuries. Three large stone crosses are built into the exterior of the church walls, two in the south wall and one in the west. Originally gravestones, these crosses were apparently taken from the churchyard in the eleventh century to be used in the reconstruction work.

A younger church, which today shares a vicar with four other parishes, is Christ Church in the medieval village of Appleton-le-Moors. Built in 1865 and described by John Betjeman as 'a little gem of moorland churches', it is in extravagant French Gothic style with a beautiful stained-glass rose window. The architect responsible was John Pearson, who also designed Truro Cathedral and who undertook the Lastingham church renovations a decade later.

Less picturesque – and, being ruined, certainly less used – is Rosedale Abbey, in the village of the same name. The abbey, or more accurately the priory, is thought to have been founded by landowner William de Rosedale in the twelfth century, for the refuge and education of the daughters of noble families. It belonged to a Cistercian order, and the nine nuns were supervised by a prioress and helped by a few farmers and shepherds. The priory was endowed with parcels of land across the moors and eventually ran large flocks of sheep, producing wool for sale.

In the fourteenth century Rosedale Abbey was visited by Archbishop Greenfield. He forbade the nuns to wear bright colours and ordered them not to let puppies enter the church to impede the devotions! In the same century marauding Scots raided Rosedale and damaged the priory so badly that the nuns moved out.

The cloister was eventually converted into small houses, the chancel was restored for use as the parish church and the convent buildings became part of a manor house described in 1649 as 'large . . . much decayed, roofed with thatch'.

In 1850 Rosedale was still one of the most complete relics of a small priory in the north of England. It stood for almost 700 years, but a stone turret with a small stair and traces of a large west window are all that remain today.

On a grander scale, on the fringes of the upland plateau, are the imposing Whitby Abbey, the soaring remains of Byland Abbey and the Mount Grace Priory near Osmotherley. This was founded by Carthusians in 1398, the monks sworn to strict vows of silence. Today their tiny cells, each with its own garden, can still be visited, and the ruins are regarded as among the finest examples of Carthusian buildings in Britain. Those are the architectural giants, certainly, but it is the moorland abbeys and churches, living and ruined, that offer a more intimate glimpse of the days when Christianity ruled the moors.

Malo Cross

WALK 5

CLEVELAND HILLS

DIFFICULTY 👢👢👢 **DISTANCE 9¼ miles (15 km)**

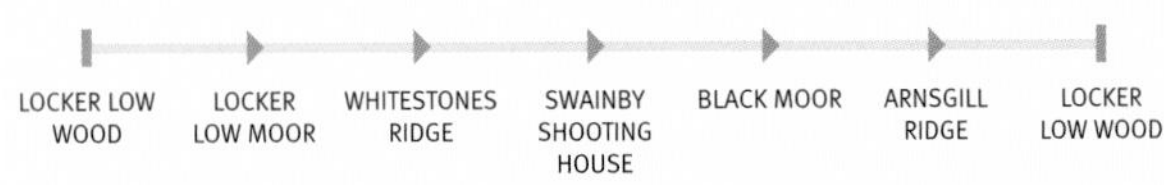

MAP OS Explorer OL26, North York Moors (Western Area)

STARTING POINT Roadside clearing with an open access information board at Locker Low Wood (GR 511944)

PUBLIC TRANSPORT The nearest point is Square Corner (Moorsbus M9 via Osmotherley). Out of Moorsbus season (see page 77) you can get as far as Osmotherley with the year-round Abbotts of Leeming route 80/89, running between Northallerton and Stokesley (call 01677 422858 for more information). Walk ¾ mile (1.2 km) south-east to join the route at point ❷.

PARKING In the clearing

A steady hike around an upland plateau on the Snilesworth estate in the Cleveland Hills. A series of linked shooting tracks gives access to panoramic views on the western escarpment of the North York Moors.

▶ From the roadside clearing, follow bridleway signs across the ford and right, up a hill and on to open moorland ❶. Cross Locker Low Moor to the deserted farmhouse of Dale Head and follow its access track to the road ❷. Then bear right across the moor to join a shooting track, to begin the gentle climb up Whitestones Ridge.

■ Pause for a moment to look over your right shoulder, for a classic view of the Tabular Hills. From this angle the hills resemble a huge plank of wood that has been tilted on to one side, creating a sort of step (known locally as a nab end) that slants off to a table-top plateau. The steep north-facing headlands, which developed when springs eroded the face of the escarpment, range in height from 500 ft (150 m) to over 1000 ft (300 m).

The Tabular Hills effectively mark the southern boundary of the national park. They are home to a long-distance walk known as the Link, which joins the start and finish points of the Cleveland Way.

▶ The track climbs up Osmotherley Moor, with views opening to the west over the Northallerton plains.

■ Just left of the track, on a high point on this section of moor, is a duo of boundary stones. This arrangement of a tall, square-cut stone, engraved with initials, standing next to an older, irregular stone which is smooth with age and weather, is common on this moor although seldom seen elsewhere.

This particular tall stone is neatly engraved with the words FABERS STONE. The initials D on the east face and M on the west refer to Lord Duncombe of Helmsley and Lord Manners; the stone marked the old boundary between their vast estates. Manners is the family name of the Dukes of Rutland, who for ten generations held Helmsley and a large area of moors before they were bought by the Duncombes in 1695. Further up the moor, opposite the Swainby Shooting House, is Nedson Stone. This carries an extra letter, A, referring to Lord Aylesbury of Snilesworth.

▸ From Fabers Stone ❸ the track is clearly visible as it continues its climb up the moor. On a broad plateau with views in all directions, it reaches a stone building ❹.

■ Swainby Shooting House is one of a handful of structures on the moor built to shelter grouse shooters from the vagaries of upland weather. It is a stone hut with a corrugated iron roof and a floor of stone slabs. A chimney and fireplace occupy one wall and daylight filters through a clear plastic panel in the roof; there are no windows. The door is

▶ Map continues northwards on pages 74–5

unlocked and the hut has obviously been used for shelter by passing walkers or estate workers. It is, however, private property.

▶ The track, now on Whorlton Moor, continues to climb and then dip towards a north-facing escarpment of the Cleveland Hills.

■ Below is the pretty valley of Scugdale, a fertile green ribbon between two upland moors. Its name means the sheltered dale, from the Danish *skygger*, to overshadow. The valley was once mined for jet and ironstone; the mines were opened in 1857 and a railway line was laid the following year to take out the iron ore. The output by 1880 was more than 66,000 tons but the lease terminated in 1887 and the mines were closed.

The area is also popular among rock climbers, with

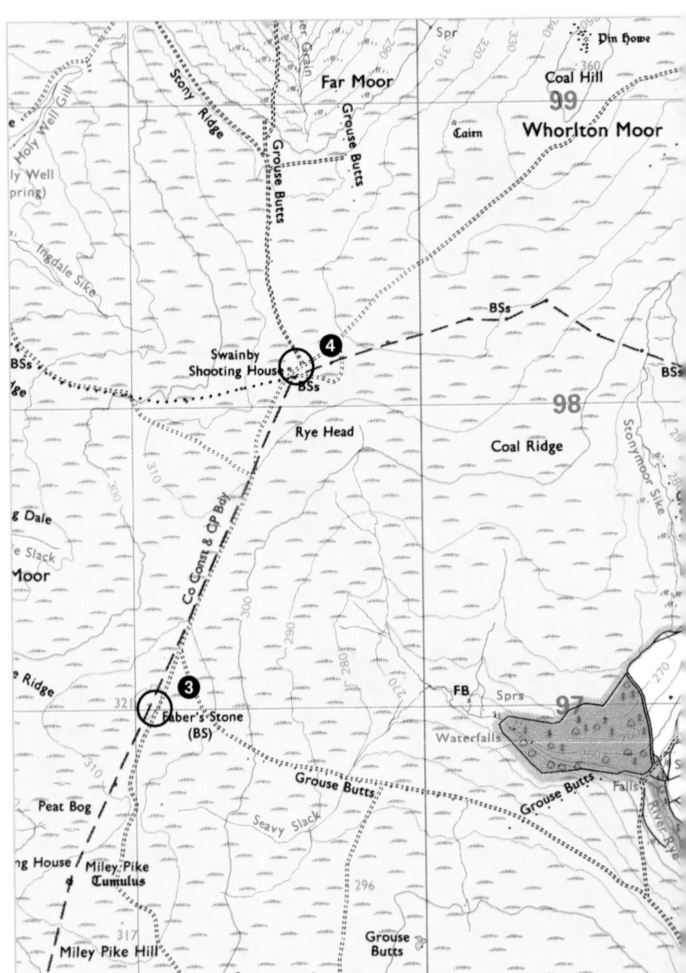

short routes and bouldering problems on the sandstone crags and buttresses. Scots Crags and Barkers Crags, clearly seen from this viewpoint, are favourites, between them offering more than 120 climbs.

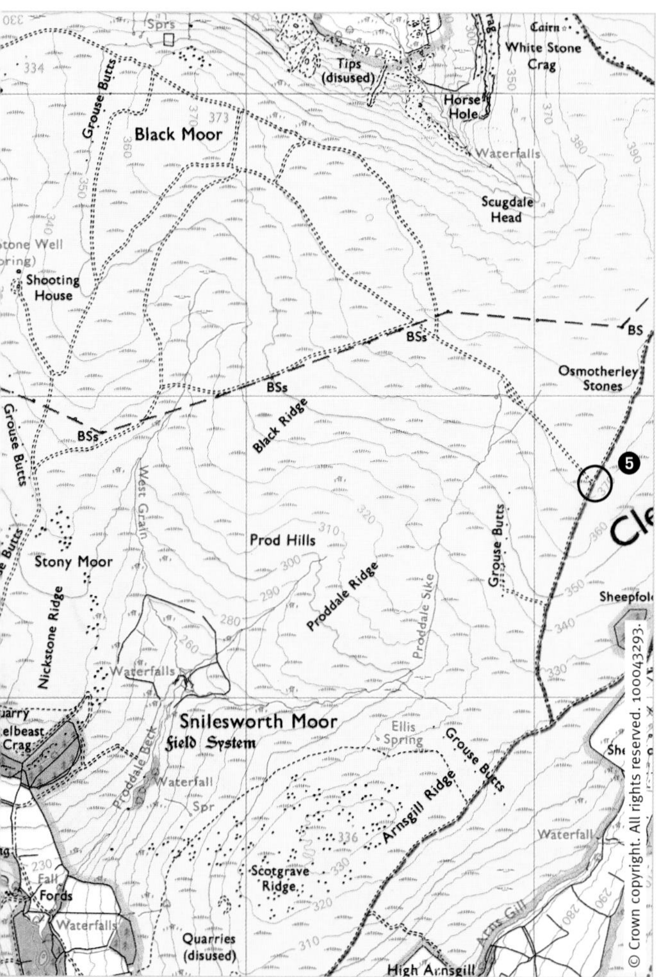

The secluded valley is famous for more than rock: its people were special as well. Records from 1890 state that Elizabeth Harland, a Scugdale resident, died in 1812 at the grand age of 105. Later in the nineteenth century Harry Cooper, reputed to be the tallest man in the world, spent some of the early years of his life as a farm servant at Scugdale Hall. This remarkable man grew 13 in (30 cm) in the space of five months, while confined to his bed. He attained the lofty height of 8 ft 6 in (2.7 m) and, at twenty-three years old, weighed 406 lb (184 kg). He accompanied the monster elephant Jumbo to America and was exhibited in Barnum's Colossal Show.

▶ Stay on the track as it curves around the head of Whorlton Moor on to Black Moor. It skirts to the south of a high point with a stone cairn and eventually loses height, to join another track above the little valley of Arns Gill ❺.

■ The moors and low ridges around Arns Gill are covered with ancient field systems. On the far side of Arns Gill is Cow Ridge, on whose western face (which you are looking at from this vantage point) a number of mesolithic flints have been found. The mesolithic period, or Middle Stone Age, began with the end of the last glacial period over 10,000 years ago. Evolution into the neolithic period involved the gradual domestication of plants and animals and the formation of settled communities at different times and places. The finds indicate that this place was visited by the earliest people to inhabit the North York Moors.

▶ Turn right here and again at the next track junction, to descend Arnsgill Ridge. This track is now a bridleway ❻. Follow it through the field systems and farmyards to the road, and turn left to return to Locker Low Wood.

Public transport: The Moorsbus

The Moorsbus has been established to reduce traffic congestion and air pollution in the North York Moors National Park. It is operated by the park authority and supported by the North Yorkshire County Council.

The Moorsbus operates on Sundays and Bank Holidays (including Good Friday and Easter Saturday), from Easter until the end of October. It runs daily during summer school holidays and extra weekday services may be offered from June to September.

Moorsbuses will pick up and drop off on request, where it is safe to do so. For full details of the route network and timetables, telephone 01845 597000 or go to www.moors.uk.net/moorsbus.

The Moorsbus network links up with several other local and long-distance bus services. Outside the Moorsbus season, contact individual service providers (details are given in walk introductions, where relevant) or ring Traveline, the public-transport information line 0870 6082608.

WALK 6

BEAUTIFUL BILSDALE

DIFFICULTY 👢👢👢👢 **DISTANCE 8 miles (13 km)**

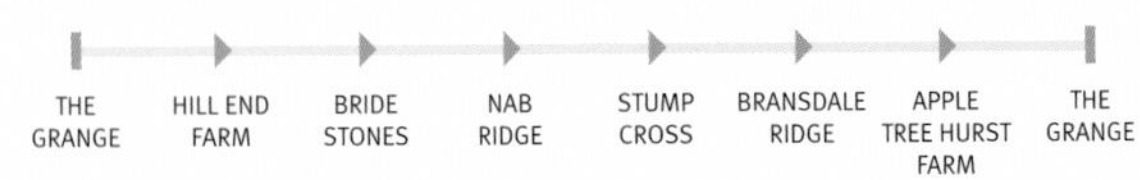

MAP OS Explorer OL26, North York Moors (Western Area)

STARTING POINT Small lay-by at The Grange, Bilsdale, on the B1257 (GR 573962)

PUBLIC TRANSPORT Moorsbus M2 (see page 77). Ask to be let off at The Grange.

PARKING In the lay-by

Old turf roads, footpaths and untracked moor combine to make an exhilarating circuit. Confident navigation is needed, and walking poles are advised, on the final section through deep heather.

▶ From the lay-by, walk north up the B1257 for 100 yards (100 m) and turn right up the footpath and access track to Hill End Farm ❶. Follow the footpath through the farmyard and bear right towards a wooden shed, continuing over a stile into a hollow way (sunken road). Follow this diagonally up a hill, through a corner of forestry and up a series of bends on to open moor, for the first views over Bilsdale.

■ The long valley of Bilsdale stretches from Stokesley south to Helmsley, through the Cleveland Hills. The River Seph snakes along its base and green fields rise to rugged moorland. A handful of tiny settlements, including Fangdale Beck and Chop Gate, punctuate the pastoral scene. The main drawback to life in this high-sided valley is the B1257, which motorcyclists use as a race track; it is known as the Bilsdale TT after the high-speed road circuit on the Isle of Man.

▶ As the hollow way approaches a dry-stone wall with a gate ❷, turn left, climb to a stile and continue straight on up the hill (keeping the high dry-stone wall to your left). A recent vehicle track offers an alternative to the hollow way up the crest of Nab Ridge, past a cluster of weathered grey stones and a tall cairn ❸.

■ There are several collections of stones known as Bride Stones on the North York Moors. Some seem to have been positioned by man in conjunction with burial mounds, others are natural outcrops weather-beaten into fantastic shapes. This group of forty-odd stones on Nab Ridge is evidence of human intervention and may have formed the retaining wall of a burial chamber whose earth covering has disappeared.

▶ Follow the track along the ridge to a junction ❹. Turn right on to a recent track alongside high bilberry banks.

■ The track running along and down the ridge is based on an old turf road, traditionally used to bring peat, turf and coal dug from the moor back to the villages (see page 84).

▶ The track twists down the hill to cross Tripsdale Beck. Climb the hill on the far side using the recent track or tracing the line of the original path via a stone enclosure and a scramble next to a small waterfall. From the top of the waterfall, bear left to the obvious 4x4 track and follow it over the moor.

■ Now a clay-topped track used by estate gamekeepers,

▶ page 82

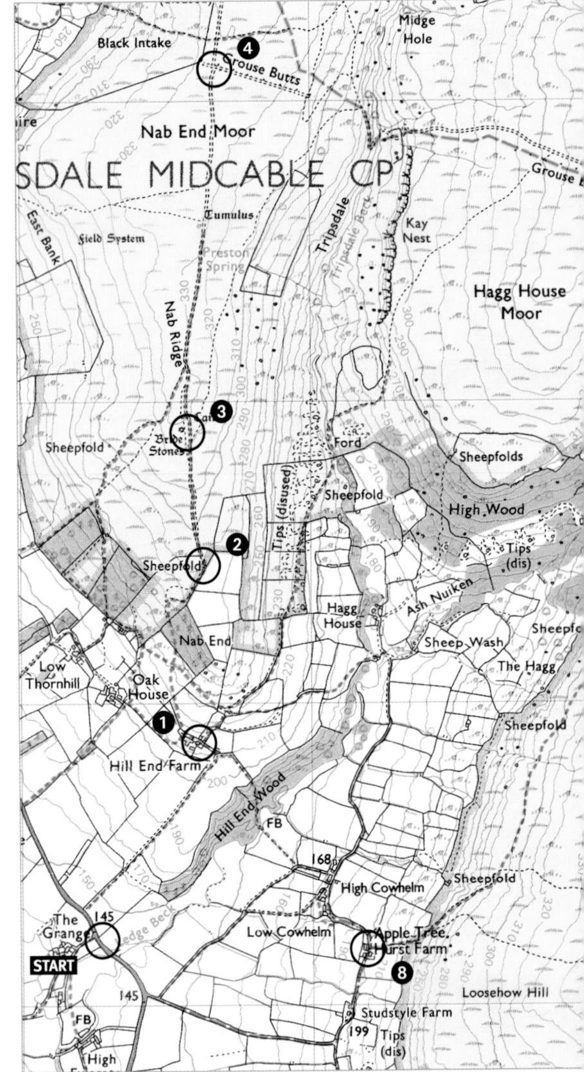
Black Intake
Grouse Butts
Midge Hole
Nab End Moor
SDALE MIDCABLE CP
Grouse
Cumulus
Field System
East Bank
Preston Spring
Tripsdale
Tripsdale Beck
Kay Nest
Hagg House Moor
Nab Ridge
Bride Stones
Sheepfold
Ford
Sheepfolds
Sheepfold
High Wood
Tips (disused)
Tips (dis)
Sheepfold
Ash Nuiken
Hagg House
Sheep Wash
The Hagg
Nab End
Low Thornhill
Oak House
Sheepfold
Hill End Farm
Hill End Wood
FB
168
High Cowhelm
Sheepfold
The Grange
145
Low Cowhelm
Apple Tree Hurst Farm
START
Loosehow Hill
145
FB
Studstyle Farm
199
Tips (dis)
High

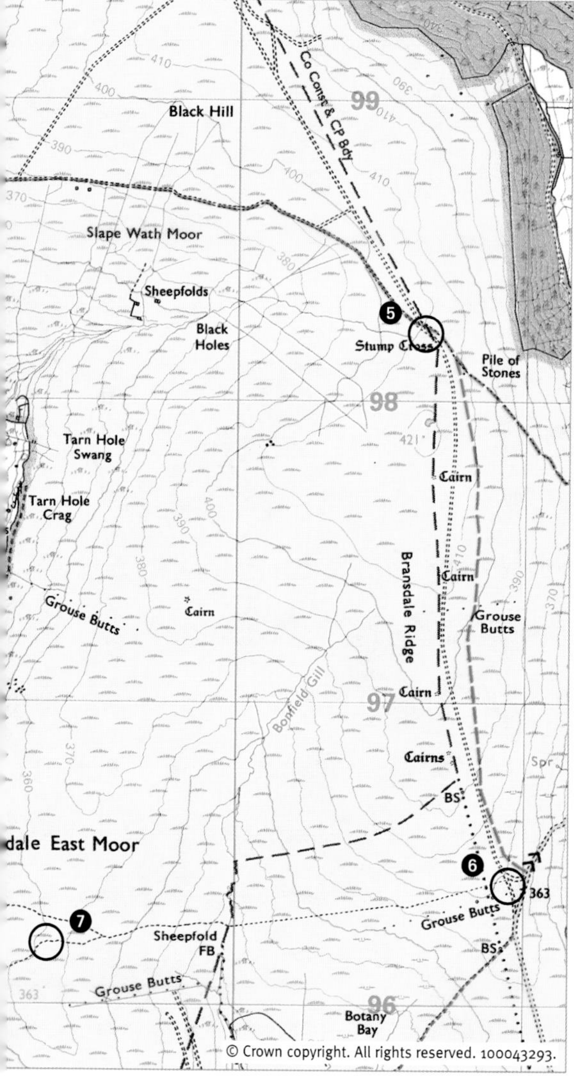

Black Hill
Co Const & CP Bdy
Slape Wath Moor
Sheepfolds
Black Holes
Stump Cross
Pile of Stones
Tarn Hole Swang
Tarn Hole Crag
Cairn
Bransdale Ridge
Grouse Butts
Bonfield Gill
Cairns
BS
dale East Moor
Sheepfold
FB
Botany Bay
363

this is the medieval Via Magna. It was described as 'the great road coming from the Thurkilsti' in a charter granting land to Rievaulx Abbey in 1145. Thurkilsti is the long track running down the line of Bransdale Ridge, one of four important roads crossing the moor from Helmsley. As you follow the Via Magna across the moor, you will pass a series of knee-high stones; these are likely to be waymarks or boundary stones, keeping travellers on the right track in bad weather.

▶ Bear right at the junction with Thurkilsti ❺, the track along Bransdale Ridge, and pass Stump Cross on your right.

■ Stump Cross (also visited in Walk 3) is a chunk of sandstone wedged into a large base, in a classic pestle and mortar arrangement. It stands just off a high point on Bransdale Ridge, with a fine view south toward Helmsley.

▶ Continue due south along the track. Just before a line of grouse butts, 100 yards (100 m) before the track joins a tarmac road, turn right on a faint path heading west ❻. Follow the line of this overgrown, ancient hollow way west-south-west, or to the left of the Bilsdale transmitting mast on the horizon, down to Bonfield Gill. At the stream, bear left to the remains of a stone sheepfold, cross the stream and work left up and across the hill, over a drainage channel, to a recently built track that climbs the moor.

At the high point of 1190 ft (363 m) the track veers north along the ridge, past a slim finger of stone. At the stone turn left ❼ and descend the moor through deep heather, towards the Bilsdale transmitting mast. At a stone cairn on the near horizon bear right, to pick up a hollow way which winds leftwards downhill. The hollow way finishes at a stone-wall field system above Apple Tree Hurst Farm.

Following a footpath marked on the map (there is no track on the ground), descend through the field above the farmhouse and over a stile to the access track ❽. Turn right to follow a bridleway through High Cow Helm farmyard and then left down its access track to the road. Alternatively, turn left on a bridleway via Studstyle Farm and then right on to the farm access track.

■ If you continued straight on at Studstyle Farm along the footpath network, you would soon arrive at the old Sun Inn, known locally as Spout House. But you'd be hard pressed to order a pint: William Ainsley, landlord, called last orders in 1914. Luckily, William Ainsley, landlord, is still serving pints at the Sun Inn across the farmyard. Confused?

The original Sun Inn is one of the area's hidden gems. Built as a farm tenant's cottage in 1550, it became a pub in 1714. Two hundred years later its popularity with local farmers, shooting parties and travelling Quakers (who regularly stopped in for afternoon tea) meant that a new, larger pub was needed. The thatched, cruck-frame alehouse closed its doors in 1914 and the new Sun Inn, just across the yard, was opened. The landlord then, as had been the case since 1823, was William Ainsley. The tradition has remained unbroken and today's pint is likely to be pulled by the latest in the William Ainsley line. The Sun Inn also has its own cricket team, which plays on a rugged pitch in the field outside the pub.

The original Sun Inn was restored and opened to the public in 1982, offering a fascinating picture of life in a simple, but special, country cottage. It is administered by the North York Moors National Park Authority and is open from Easter to October (except Thursdays). The new Sun Inn is open most days from 11 am (no food served).

▶ The two access tracks meet just before the road. At the road, turn right and walk 100 yards (100 m) back to the start point in The Grange's lay-by.

Burning issues

Each winter through to early spring, dark smoke billows from the North York Moors. Not all over; no, control is tight. But from certain corners, over selected pieces of moorland, the air will taste black and brittle.

The reason? Fires, usually under the supervision of a gamekeeper or moorkeeper, which have been set to keep the moor in a healthy, productive condition. Between November and March small patches of heather are burned on an eight-to-fifteen-year cycle to make a mosaic of heather of different heights. The short heather provides habitat for the nesting and feeding of birds such as red grouse, golden plover and lapwing, while the longer heather is selected by the merlin.

As the burning destroys over-mature heather, it allows new growth to generate from roots and seeds. Without it, much of the moors, which 5000 years ago were covered in forest, would eventually return to woodland, with heather a minor part of the ground flora.

Fires are planned to cover small areas, move with the wind and burn old growth while doing little more than scorch the ground below. Factors which dictate when and where the fires can be set include the moisture content of the ground, which for the most part is made up of peat beds. Unfortunately, however, not all fires are set under supervision and not all are controlled. Damage from a spate of major fires, accidental or arson, in 1976 can still be seen on the moors; given the area's dependence on grouse shooting and sheep grazing, these had serious repercussions for the fragile upland and its economy.

Small-scale, managed burning has always been an integral part of moorland management. But it's not just about the heather: what's underneath it counts too. The dark, damp beds of peat and turf underlying the heather have provided major sources of fuel for centuries. After the moors have burnt, the hollow ways – sunken roads which splice the heather upland – become easier to see. These are turf roads, traditionally used to bring peat, turf and coal dug from the moor back to the villages.

Some people had turf rights attached to their property; others paid 'turfgraste'. The usual time for digging was in spring, after the moor had been burnt off. The turf was pared from the moor with a heavy spade, which had a winged blade and a long T-handled shaft. Rectangular chunks of turf were propped on their ends to dry, then piled into heaps known as rooks.

In summer, between hay time and harvest, the dry turf was brought down from the moor on sleds. It burned slowly, which is why the stories of 'fires that never go out' are credible (see page 148). Fires that needed encouragement were fed cowls or gowldans, the dried stalks of tall ling heather which were usually gathered two years after the moor was burnt off and made excellent kindling.

Turf was relatively easy to get hold of but peat, dug from deep bogs, was also commonly used. It dried more slowly than turf and burned at a lower temperature, but location was all: if a peat bog was nearer to you than a turf site, peat would be your fuel for winter.

Peat workings – and some, between Glaisdale and Rosedale, are still in use – were concentrated near becks, or streams. A peat face, or breast, could be 10 feet (3 metres) deep. Like turf, peat was cut in large bricks and dried on the moor, before being hauled off in late summer. In common with turf, peat was built into intricate stacks, with the highest layer shaped like a roof for water to slide off. Sometimes, the stacks were thatched with ling.

The moor also yielded many other useful treasures. Ling heather was used for kindling, thatching and besoms. These were very functional brushes, used to sweep lawns and paths. To make a besom, a large bunch of ling was compressed, then bound to a hazelwood handle with strips of ash; the result looked a little like a witch's broomstick. Sphagnum moss, from which peat eventually forms, was also collected, for dressing wounds. Bilberries and cranberries were gathered for food, and bracken was harvested for thatching and stock bedding.

Today, moss is used by nurseries to wrap and protect plants,

heather is baled and exported for use in water filtration, and bracken is useless and the scourge of the moors. And bilberries? These delicacies are enjoyed by birds and humans alike. If you are offered bilberry pie, accept immediately: it will have taken someone back-breaking hours to collect enough of the tiny purple berries to make a meal.

Heather burning on the moors

WALK 7

WAINSTONES AND ROUND HILL

DIFFICULTY 🥾🥾🥾 **DISTANCE 9¼ miles (15 km)**

MAP OS Explorer OL26, North York Moors (Western Area)

STARTING POINT Chop Gate car park (GR 559993)

PUBLIC TRANSPORT Moorsbus M2, M9 (see page 77)

PARKING In the car park

Ancient earthworks, the Cleveland Way, sweeping views and a rock-climbers' corner: enjoy them all on this diverse circuit around the head of Bilsdale.

▶ Climb the stile in the south-west corner of the car park and follow the footpath waymarks across fields. Once over the tarmac Raisdale Road, cross more fields and take the right fork heading uphill. This emerges on Cold Moor Lane, a sunken track between stone walls ❶. Turn left and continue through a series of double gates, on to the open moor.

■ The village below is called Chop Gate (the name is pronounced Chop Yat), and it is the only settlement of any size in Bilsdale. It has a school, a pub (one of only two in the valley), a public car park with toilets and a village hall. At the northern end is Seave Green, almost an extension of Chop Gate.

The pretty church of St Hilda sits on a hillside above Seave Green, with beautiful views over the valley. Built in 1851, it occupies the site of a much earlier building dating back to around 1170. The original foundation stone can still be seen, built into the porch of the new church. Inside, the medieval font and pieces of the original stone window frames survive.

▶ Make your way across and up the moor, aiming for the high point and three barely visible howes, or burial mounds ❷. The easiest route is on a bridleway, but the whole of Cold Moor is yours to explore.

■ If you're standing on the top and looking west, you will see a large building on the skyline, an incongruous sight in an otherwise empty moor. This is the Carlton Moor Gliding Club, above Carlton Bank. It was founded in 1931 as the Newcastle Gliding Club. At that time, most of the flying was carried out at Sunderland Airport, which is now the location of the Nissan car factory.

The club moved to its present site on the North York Moors in the early 1960s, and was renamed the Newcastle and Teesside Gliding Club. More recently the club changed its name again, to reflect its location. It is a relatively small and very friendly club, and gliders can be seen soaring over the moors on most weekends.

▶ Continue along, down and up the long ridge in front of you.

■ Directly ahead, framed by the moor and the Wainstones, is the unmistakable profile of Roseberry Topping. It is known as the Matterhorn of the moors – although it is a fairly squashed Matterhorn, given the flattened summit.

▶ From here you can either climb to the high point directly ahead or pick up a bridleway that cuts across and down the hill. Either way, you will arrive at windy Garfit Gap, directly below the Wainstones ❸.

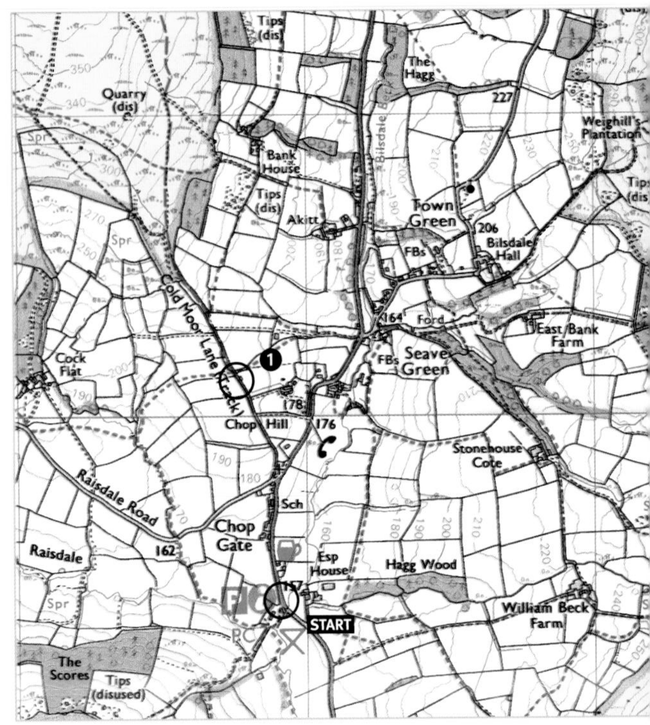

■ The Wainstones are a glorious jumble of stacked and toppled rocks, on the edge of Hasty Bank. This is a particularly enjoyable place to rock climb, with a winning combination of views and easy-to-grip sandstone.

According to the book published by the Cleveland Mountaineering Club, *Rock Climbs on the North York Moors*, the first climber to explore here was E.E. Roberts in 1906, although he wrote: 'odd visits don't count, some idle shepherd boy may have climbed here before me'. He was followed before the First World War by, among others,

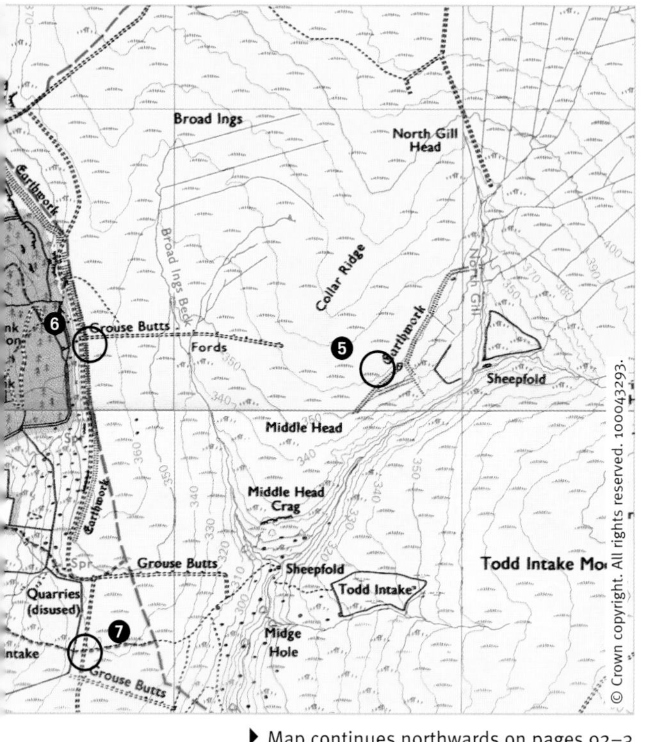

▸ Map continues northwards on pages 92–3

the Creighton brothers, who cycled from York to climb here, a round journey of more than 80 miles (130 km). One of the brothers continued visiting during the First World War, when, armed with a revolver, he patrolled the rocks in the dark 'looking for Zeppelins'.

▸ Climb through the Wainstones to the top of Hasty Bank (either on the footpath or by nipping up Ling Buttress, a route of 30 ft (9 m) graded Severe . . .). Follow the paved path down to the B1257 and continue up the other side, following Cleveland Way waymarks. Stay on the Cleveland Way, passing numerous boundary

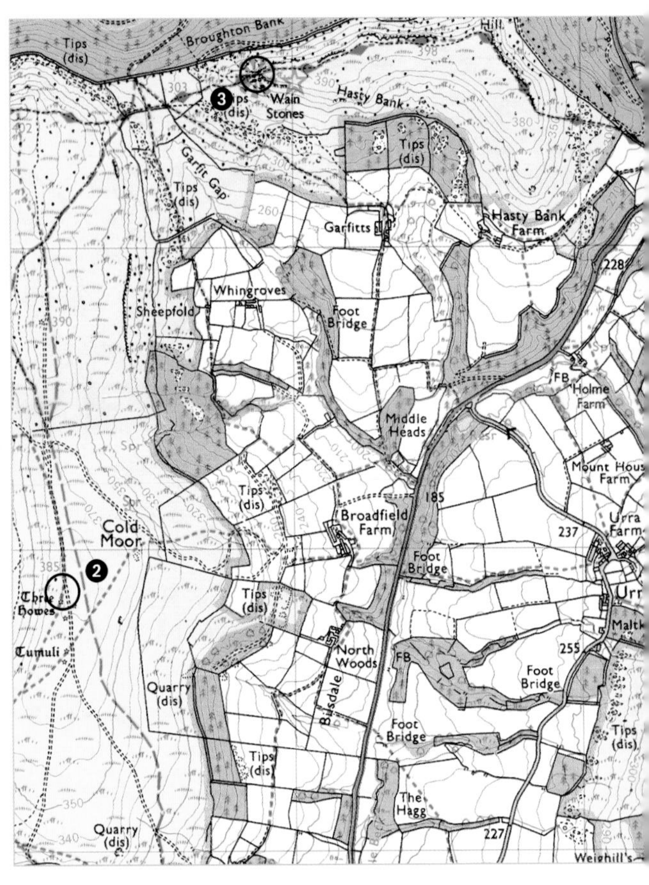

stones and cairns, on the steady climb to Round Hill ❹.

■ At 1489 ft (454 m), Round Hill is the highest point on the North York Moors. At its top is a tumulus, a fitting place for a burial with views in all directions. From its trig point, you can clearly see a dark diagonal slash across the hillside to the east. This

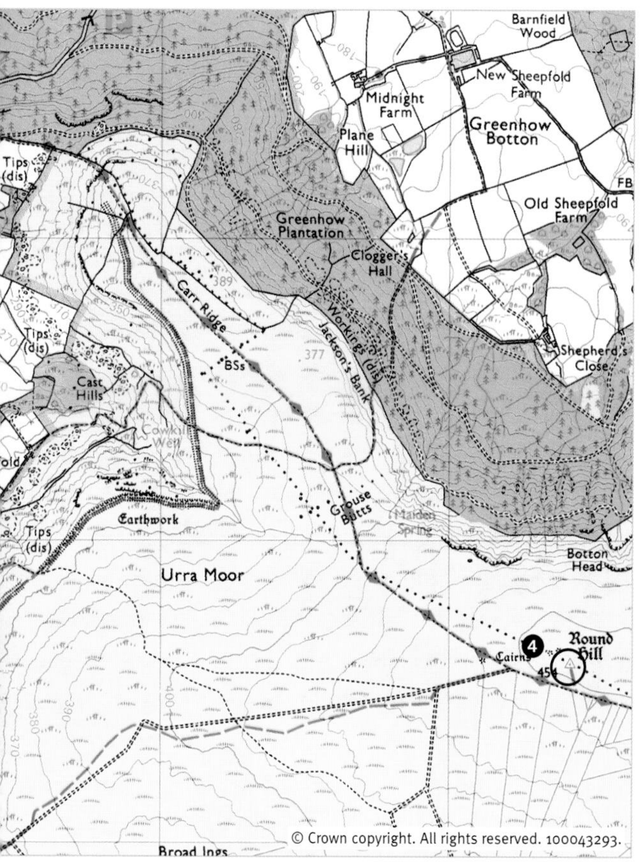

is Ingleby Incline (visited in Walk 3), a vital part of the railway line built in the nineteenth century to transport iron ore from Rosedale, two valleys away.

▶ Backtrack slightly to a path heading west and, after a few minutes, turn left. (If walking over rough heather does not appeal, do not turn left. Stay on this path and turn left on the escarpment.)

When the path swings right, continue on down and across the moor, on the general line of Collar Ridge. When the ridge begins to flatten, look for the remains of a sunken track; it is thoroughly overgrown but the line is still visible ❺.

The old track coincides with a line of circular, sunken, stone grouse butts covered with bilberries, and is also on the same line as a track you can see climbing the hill to the west. Follow the track until it arrives on an escarpment ❻.

Bilsdale from the Wainstones

■ This ancient earthwork of ditches and banks runs for about 3 miles (5 km) along the rim of Urra Moor. Its origins are unknown, but in this area dykes of banks and ditches, like this one, usually marked boundaries.

▶ Turn left and follow the track along the escarpment. When it turns left, bear right and follow the edge of a dry-stone wall to a gate ❼. Go through the gate and follow the footpath network through William Beck Farm, back to the car park.

Walking on history

Look carefully, along the line of the moor. See that dull glint in the heather, almost smothered by gnarled roots? It's a stone causeway, fat slabs weathered by centuries, pounded by hooves and feet. These stone routes are everywhere, criss-crossing the high plateau of the moors, alongside modern roads, across fields, through forests. A treat to discover, they are also a delight to walk on, as many cover areas of moor that are wet or boggy.

The system is complex and extensive. Many stone tracks date from medieval times, other routes can be traced to neolithic days, while some are trade roads developed in the Bronze and Iron Ages. The majority are likely to have been laid under instruction from the religious orders, who needed to travel between the abbeys and their outlying farms, sheepfolds and fisheries. The bulk of construction was probably undertaken in the fourteenth century around the time of the Black Death, when consistently foul weather turned the moors to marsh.

Origins aside, the causeways really came into their own in the seventeenth century. Charcoal and coal, ironstone and lime, wool and cloth had to be hauled, year round, across the plateau, and stone paths were the only way to keep the packhorses moving. In places where there were no hard-topped causeways, such as around Saltersgate on the eastern moors, the pack trains sank into the mud and the deep, rutted tracks that were formed are still visible today.

The raw material used to create the hard roads was sandstone, which was relatively easily quarried into thick, square slabs. Sandstone is soft, in contrast to the gritstone used for causeways in the south Pennines, and centuries of use by ponies and people wore depressions into the slabs.

The stone tracks were used by all comers. There are monks' ways, Quakers' causeways, smugglers' paths, panniermen's tracks and church and mill ways. Some are marked on contemporary maps, but others have fallen entirely out of use.

One of the best examples of a stone walkway is the George Gap Causeway, which runs from Rosedale Head over the wild moors north-east to Great Fryup Head. It becomes Long Causeway as it drops through the dale, leading eventually to Lealholm. Parts are named Quakers' Trod and the Old Pannier Track. Another superb section is the Quakers' Causeway above Commondale (see Walk 8). Well-preserved trods can also be found in Arnecliff Wood near Glaisdale and in lower Eskdale. Many lead to medieval bridges, as in Westerdale, Danby and the Esk valley. Old churches also tend to have causeways leading to them, like spokes to a hub. Four causeways converge from the points of the compass on the church at Danby, while the churches at Rosedale, Goathland, Egton, Glaisdale and Ingleby are also visited by stone paths.

Not all travellers on the causeways had the fine intentions of the monks. Smugglers' trods zigzag across the moors, including the route that crosses Commondale Beck to Gin Garth in Westerdale (perhaps the old rumours of an illicit gin still were true). This remains one of the area's most remote dales, so a modern-day smuggler would likely carry on his trade in peace.

Mill ways were shorter, used as local routes around the corn mills, rather than as long-distance highways. Mills at Goathland, Lealholm and Castleton have fine examples.

As mill wheels turn so time spins too, and eventually the stone tracks became outdated. Roads were built and surfaced with limestone, and the pack trains left the moor tops. But the causeways remain, their worn stones offering rescue to walkers who would otherwise flounder in the peaty bogs. To be struggling up a moor and see in front a long line of stone slabs is to experience the feelings of a desert traveller stumbling into an oasis. But these stones are not a mirage – they are a symbol of travellers past. Tread with care; you are stepping on history.

WALK 8

COMMONDALE

DIFFICULTY **DISTANCE 6¾ miles (11 km)**

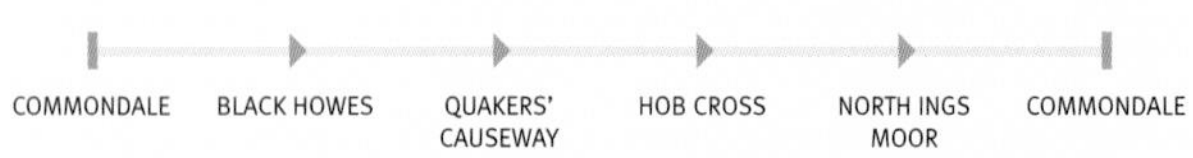

MAP OS Explorer OL26, North York Moors (Western Area)

STARTING POINT Commondale (GR 662105)

PUBLIC TRANSPORT There is a railway station at Commondale on the line between Middlesbrough and Whitby (www.eskvalleyrailway.co.uk).

PARKING On the roadside at the starting point

A mix of rough moorland, farm tracks and a stone-paved causeway lead you up and over this northernmost section of the North York Moors. Navigation skills will be needed.

▸ From Commondale's main road, running parallel with the railway line, walk east up the hill with the Cleveland Inn on your right.

■ It is immediately apparent that Commondale is not one of your quaint moorland villages. For a start, red brick rather than traditional stone is used in many of the buildings, the church of St Peter and the old school house being obvious examples. But you use what you've got, and until the 1950s Commondale had its own brickworks. The village may not be that pretty, but it boasts a tea room, a pub and public toilets, which are all a walker really needs.

▸ Once past the red-brick church, climb the hill to a new wooden gate in a wire fence ❶. Go through the gate up the moor to a stone enclosure with the remains of a forest plantation. Walk through this to the north-east corner and continue through the wooden gate on to open moor ❷.

■ The tall stone to the right of the gate is a boundary stone, engraved RC 1798. The initials refer to Robert Chaloner, Lord of the Manor and Member of Parliament for York. His ancestor Sir Thomas Chaloner purchased Guisborough in 1547.

▸ The line of boundary stones continues over the moor and the route meets up with them at its northernmost point, by Hobb Cross. While you are free to walk anywhere on this moor, it tends to be boggy with hidden ditches and deep heather. In the early stages of the walk, following the established paths is your best option.

Follow the line of boundary stones up the moor, then bear off right along the obvious path. This leads to the tarmac Smeathorns Road. Stay left and pick up a bridleway running north-west over the moor ❸.

■ Ahead is the North Sea, usually busy with container ships and trawlers. Much nearer at hand is a smooth green dome, quite at odds with the landscape around it. This is Hagg Hill, thought to be the core of an eroded volcano, one of several on the North York Moors. Although evidence of volcanic activity is not common on the moors, Cliff Ridge and Langbaurgh Ridge, just north of Great Ayton, are nearby examples of basaltic dykes. The British Tertiary Volcanic Province was active over a period of about eleven million years, largely during the Palaeocene epoch, 65–56.5 million years ago.

▸ The bridleway runs past several low tumuli. These are the Bronze Age burial mounds known as Black Howes.

▸ page 102

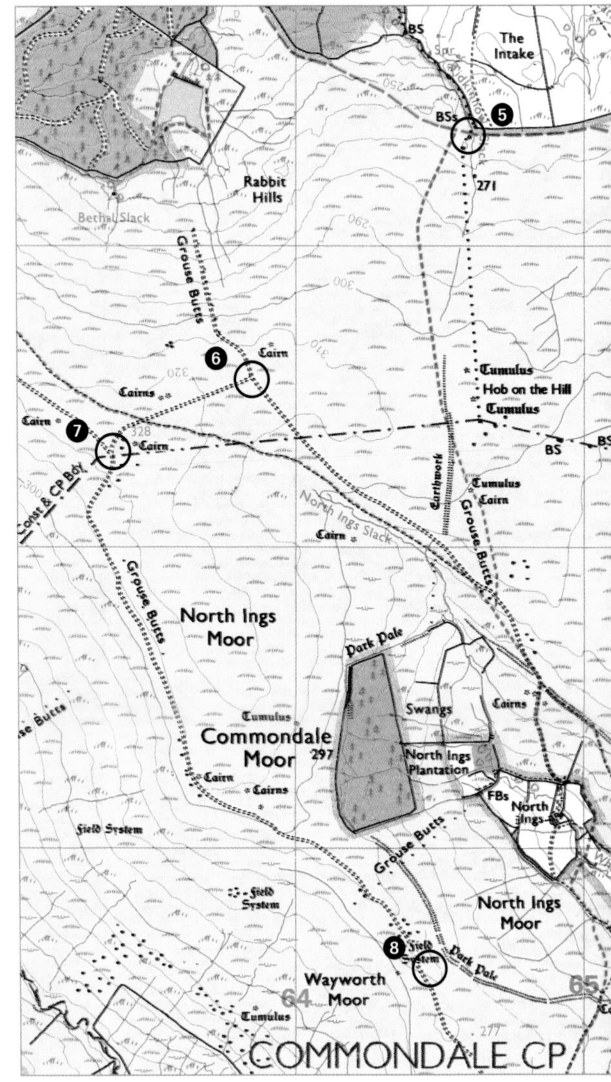
The Intake
Rabbit Hills
Bethal Slack
Grouse Butts
Cairn
Cairns
Cumulus
Hob on the Hill
Earthwork
North Ings Slack
Const & CP Bdy
North Ings Moor
Park Pale
Swangs
North Ings Plantation
Commondale Moor
Field System
Wayworth Moor
COMMONDALE CP

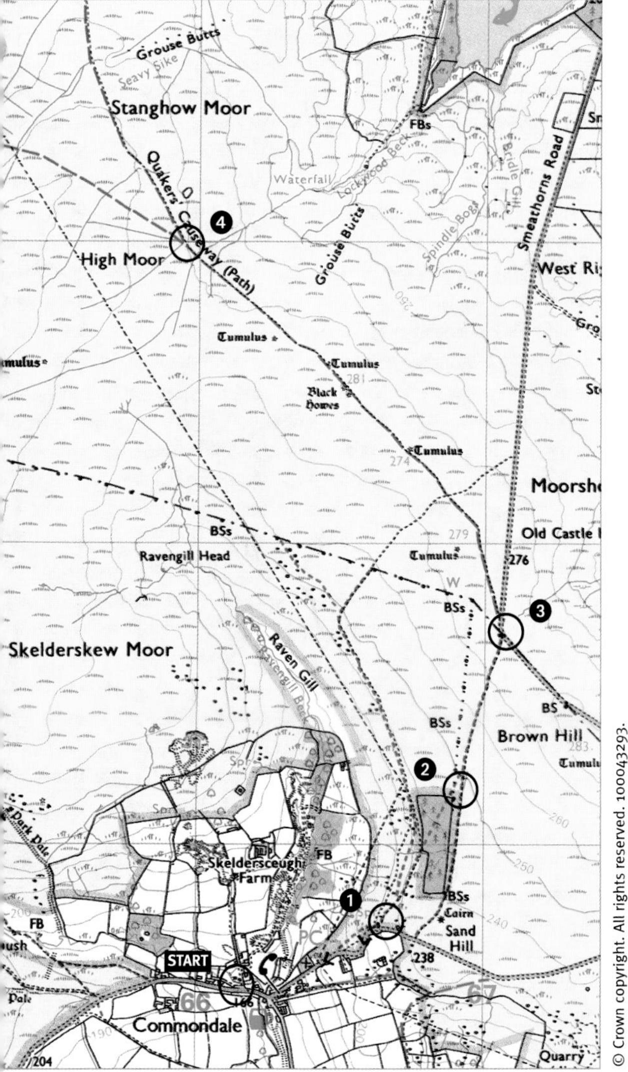

Grouse Butts
Seavy Sike
Stanghow Moor
FBs
Lockwood Beck
Waterfall
Bridle Gill
Smeathorns Road
Quakers Causeway (Path)
4
High Moor
Grouse Butts
Spindle Bogs
West Ri
Tumulus
Tumulus
281
Black Howes
Tumulus
274
Moorsh
BSs
279
Old Castle
Ravengill Head
Tumulus
276
BSs
3
Skelderskew Moor
Raven Gill
Ravengill Beck
BS
BSs
Brown Hill
283
Tumulu
2
260
Park Dale
FB
Skelderskeugh Farm
250
1
BSs
Cairn
Sand Hill
240
FB
START
238
PC
166
Commondale
190
204
Quarry

Soon the path turns into a stone-paved causeway.

■ This is the Quakers' Causeway, one of the best examples of stone-paved tracks on the North York Moors. Its full length extends from Aysdale Gate near Guisborough to White Cross at Commondale, although the stone slabs disappear at Black Howes. The causeway, also called a trod, is made from sandstone and provided a safe, relatively dry crossing over the boggy moor. There are many such routes over these moors, most thought to have been built in the fourteenth century when monastic expansion, and therefore increased moorland traffic, combined with deteriorating weather conditions and an increasingly marshy moor (see page 96). This particular path is likely to have been used later as a route between Quaker meeting houses.

▶ At a footpath marker on High Moor bear left ❹ and follow the path to the end of a dry-stone wall.

■ The view from this point is of the belching chimney stacks and factories of Middlesbrough. The juxtaposition of this industrial town against the serenity of the moors, with its wind-brushed heather and whistling curlews, emphasizes how lucky we are to enjoy open access. It also shows how this truly is the northern edge of the North York Moors: from here, it's downhill to the industrial sprawl and the sea.

▶ Turn left and climb the nearby mound crowned with a tall stone ❺.

■ This is the shaft of Hob Cross, which doubles as a boundary stone in the RC 1798 line crossed earlier. The mound is not a tumulus but formed from gravel and sand left by a retreating glacier during the last Ice Age. Hob was a local folklore character, probably an elf. There are around twenty places on the moors associated with Hobs, including a boundary stone a little to the south, between two tumuli, called Hob on the Hill.

▶ From the mound take a compass bearing south-west, over the moor. You are aiming for a track junction on the far ridge ❻. The footpath marked on the map does not exist on the ground and a bearing is the safest way to cross this section.

If you are on the right line, you will approach the ridge with a small stone cairn on your right and a track T-junction directly in front. If the track rises to your left, turn left to find the junction and then turn right down it. If the main track rises to your right, turn right and then left. Having made the turn, follow this track past several stones painted at time of writing 'No Public Right of Way'.

■ Ahead a tall monument, rising from woodland, is silhouetted against the sky. This is the Captain Cook Monument, erected to honour the eighteenth-century navigator and explorer who lived in this region until he was twenty-four. At Great Ayton, below the monument, is the Captain Cook Schoolroom Museum, the baby of the Captain Cook Tourism Association. They have established a walk of 30 miles (48 km) from Cook's birthplace in Marton-in-Cleveland, via his school at Great Ayton, to Whitby where his illustrious sea-faring career began. The literal highlight of Captain Cook Country is a walk to the monument, a finger of stone 51 ft (15.5 m) high on Easby Moor.

▶ As the moor begins to descend into Sleddale, bear left at a junction ❼ (past another 'No Public Right of Way' stone) and follow the track across and down North Ings Moor. Pass through a wooden gate and descend the ridge to the lowest point, then turn east over untracked moor ❽. You will soon meet a line of ancient earthworks, a long, raised bank covered with bilberries. Follow this down the rough moor until it meets a farm access track. Turn right, and then left on to the road, heading back to the start.

The Captain Cook Monument

WALK 9

HISTORY ON DANBY RIGG

DIFFICULTY 👢👢 **DISTANCE** 5 miles (8 km)

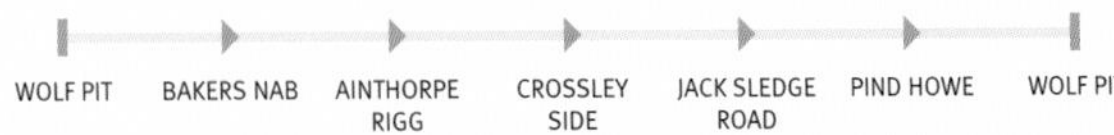

MAP OS Explorer OL26, North York Moors (Western Area)

STARTING POINT Wolf Pit, on the unclassified road from Blakey Ridge to Danby (GR 705036)

PUBLIC TRANSPORT Moorsbuses M1, M2, M3 (see page 77) run to Ainthorpe or the Moors Centre at Danby. Alternatively, take the Esk Valley Railway to Danby station on the Middlesbrough–Whitby line (www.eskvalleyrailway.co.uk), then continue by road and footpath links to join the walk at point ❸. This adds up to 1¼ miles (2 km) to the route.

PARKING On roadside at starting point

A short walk around Danby High Moor on rarely used tracks, some dating back at least six millennia. The route passes ancient field systems, standing stones and burial mounds, with views over moorland and valleys to the sea.

▶ From Wolf Pit, take the bridleway running north-west towards Botton. Just before it drops over the western escarpment of Danby Rigg, turn right and pick up a tiny path heading north ❶. This is marked on the OS map as Rake's Way and overlooks Danby Dale.

■ Danby Dale is a pretty green valley probing south from the River Esk. The Rosedale monks traversed it on their way to Whitby Abbey and, later, Quaker families settled here, away from the suspicion of the towns. They drained the land and walled the pasture, and a ribbon of farms appeared along the dale. Today these fields and houses are worked and lived in by a truly special community: Botton Village, half of whose inhabitants have special needs.

Botton Village was established in 1955 as part of the Camphill Community, which had been created in Scotland during the Second World War by refugees from Nazi-held Austria. Their leader, Dr Karl König, had been inspired by the teaching of Rudolf Steiner to seek a new understanding of children with mental disabilities and to provide the care and education they require.

The ideal of a village community, in which everyone could do meaningful work and be supported by friends who would help them realize their potential, was made possible when the MacMillan family, who owned Botton Hall, committed their home to the cause. Since the first group moved there in 1955, Botton Village has grown to include more than 300 inhabitants with five individually managed biodynamic farms. Everyone works, either on the farms and in the gardens, or producing candles, engraved glass, woven goods, bread and dairy products. In short, the community provides for each other's needs and fulfils the demands of the wider world for Botton's unique products. The village is almost completely self-contained with a shop, sawmill, granary, dairy, coffee shop, post office, theatre and school, among other enterprises, and visitors are welcome.

▶ The path winds along the edge of a rocky outcrop, passing

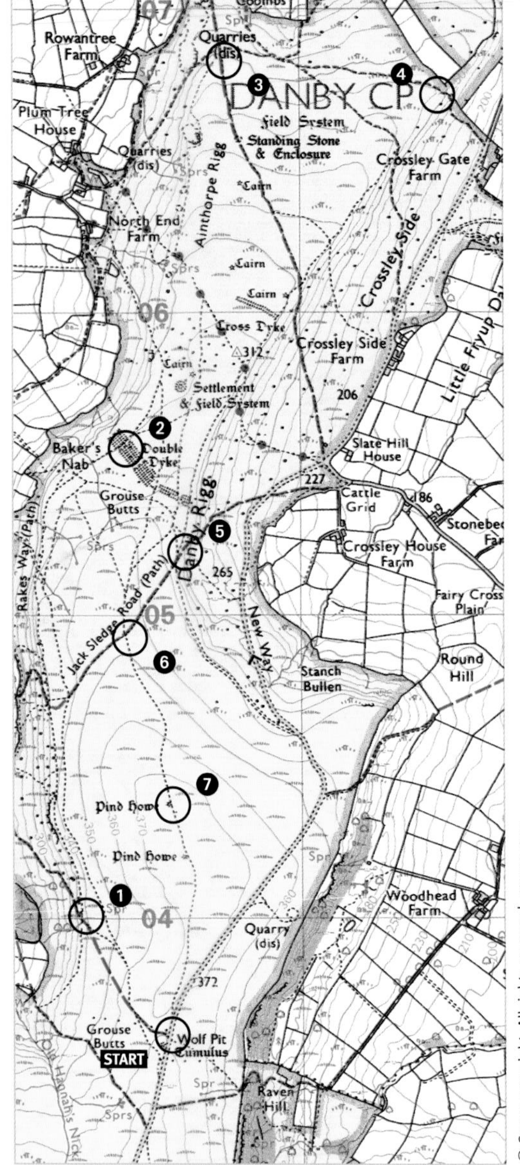
Coombs
Rowantree Farm
Quarries (dis)
DANBY CP
Plum Tree House
Field System
Standing Stone & Enclosure
Quarries (dis)
Ainthorpe Rigg
Crossley Gate Farm
Cairn
North End Farm
Crossley Side
Cairn
Cairn
Cross Dyke
Crossley Side Farm
Little Fryup Dale
312
Cairn
Settlement & Field System
206
Baker's Nab
Double Dyke
Slate Hill House
227
Grouse Butts
Danby Rigg
Cattle Grid
186
Stonebeck
Crossley House Farm
265
Rakes Way (Path)
Jack Sledge Road (Path)
Fairy Cross Plain
New Way
Round Hill
Stanch Bullen
Pind Howe
Pind Howe
Woodhead Farm
Quarry (dis)
372
Grouse Butts
START
Wolf Pit Cumulus
Raven Hill
Old Hannah's Nick
1
2
3
4
5
6
7

numerous sunken lanes, known as hollow ways. Many of these were turf roads (see page 84).

■ The sandstone cliffs and rock buttresses below make up Danby Crag, a haunt of rock climbers. More than fifty routes, varying from 20 ft (6 m) to 30 ft (9 m) in height, are graded from Difficult to Hard Very Severe. Many were created in the mid-1970s by members of the Northumberland Mountaineering Club. Rock climbing has taken place on the outcrops of North Yorkshire since 1906, although many routes are notorious for vegetation and dampness.

▶ The path almost disappears as it follows a curve in the ridge, past the series of deep ditches and banks which make up Danby's ancient Double Dyke ❷.

■ Just past the dykes, to the east, is the site of a neolithic settlement with field systems. There is little visible on the ground but some of the remains date back around 6500 years. The neolithic people who moved into the area from continental Europe chose high ground like Danby Rigg because the woodland was not as thick as on the lower slopes and the ground was less boggy. The site also would have given good views of the surrounding area, allowing advance warning of attack.

Evidence of this early population can be seen all over Danby Rigg. Heaps of stone with stone walls in between are known as cairnfields. The heaps were created when stones were cleared from the fields, and the walls are ancient field boundaries. Dykes of banks and ditches, including the one you just passed, would have marked boundaries.

▶ The path now descends, still along the escarpment, with views to the west over Danby Dale and the village of Castleton.

■ Clearly visible below you is Danby's Church of St Hilda.

Built on the site of a pre-Christian burial ground, this fascinating church incorporates Saxon and Norman remains, a fifteenth-century tower and a Victorian chancel. A gallery built in 1806 houses an organ, and is accessed by external stone steps. Inside, fresh flowers complement soaring pillars and arches, and six named stained-glass windows. St Hilda is depicted in the Missionary window. Records show that a church dedicated to her has occupied this magnificent site since 1100. The view today is quintessentially English, the stone church being surrounded by yew trees and a graveyard which contains listed tombs and headstones.

▸ The next landmark is a line of tall stones which marks an ancient road across the moor. Pass them, losing height gradually, until the path meets a bridleway running north–south along the ridge ❸. Below is a gate with an open access information board.

■ Directly below is Ainthorpe, one of the oldest villages in the area, whose green sports a quoits pitch (see page 114). Its neighbour, a hop across the River Esk and clearly seen from this point, is Danby. This village is home to the Moors Centre, one of the main information points for the North York Moors National Park. The centre is housed in Danby Lodge, a glorious property of locally quarried sandstone, which was developed from a seventeenth-century farmhouse. Besides offering books, walk leaflets and other local information, the Moors Centre has tea rooms, a wildflower garden, a large lawn with a picnic area and a woodland garden accessible to wheelchairs. It is open daily from March to December and on weekends in January and February.

▸ Cross the bridleway and head east across the hill on a narrow footpath. Continue straight on at a waymark post, then bear right up the hill at an indistinct junction of paths.

■ Below you is Danby Castle, built in the fourteenth century by the local lord, William Latimer. The castle had a commanding position at the heart of the manor of Danby, but was never intended as a fortification. Set around an inner courtyard, the castle had no keep but was built with strong outer walls and angled towers at the four corners. Today the ruined castle is part of a working farm, the farmhouse an extension of the south-west tower. In the sixteenth century, the lady of the manor was Catherine Parr, who was to become the sixth and last wife of Henry VIII. Local legends say that when Henry came to visit he was forced to shelter from the weather at a farm now called Stormy Hall, part of the Botton Village community.

▶ This footpath soon dives off the eastern escarpment of Danby Rigg. Just before it does so, turn right ❹ and pick up a small path running south-west along the edge. The path crosses a barely visible dyke, a trig point (1023 ft/312 m) with a tall marker stone, and a second dyke, to arrive at a track junction marked by a small cairn ❺.

If you have no desire to walk across deep, untracked heather, continue straight on along the escarpment and turn right up the tarmac road to the start. Otherwise, turn right up the path known as Jack Sledge Road. At a high point, just before a small cairn, turn left ❻. Make your way through heather, which can reach waist height, towards a finger of stone on the near horizon. From the stone, bear left towards a tumulus called Pind Howe ❼.

Just before the tumulus, pick up the faint line of a sunken track. Follow this towards the horizon and over the moor to the starting point. If you tire of the deep heather, cut left at any point to join the road.

Danby Dale from Castleton Rigg

Games people play

This is sporting country. The people of the North York Moors have for centuries indulged their competitive spirit, be it at cricket, hunting, growing gooseberries or playing board games. While 'sports' such as cock fighting and badger baiting have long been outlawed, other, less contentious, traditional leisure activities are still enjoyed.

Cricket remains a summer favourite. At one time virtually all the moorland villages had cricket pitches, and, while many have reverted to grazing for sheep, some pitches remain. On weekends in the cricket season, walkers on ridges which overlook villages such as Danby can easily hear the thwack of bat on ball and see tiny figures in white zooming around the greens.

Less common but still played is quoits, a game centred around Eskdale on the northern moors and dominated by the Danby and District Quoits League. Originally, quoits were made from two horseshoes forged together by a blacksmith, and they were thrown on pitches at farms, near the village inn or outside the blacksmith's shop. In the 1850s quoits teams had twelve members, which was reduced to eleven before the Second World War and later to nine. The rules of quoits are numerous and complex, with impenetrable terminology, types of throw and scoring possibilities. Although quoits continues to be played with skill and concentration, matches are now social gatherings rather than fever-pitch competitions.

Less difficult, and less frequently seen, is a game known as the bull ring. A ring is tied to a long string and swung to hook on a cow's horn fixed to a wall or post. It could be played anywhere, but today is most easily found at the Ryedale Folk Museum at Hutton-le-Hole.

Another traditional game, with roots that run deeper than quoits or bull ring, is merrills, a board game for two people.

One of the oldest-known games still played today, merrills was probably brought to England by the Normans and by the fourteenth century had become one of the most popular games in the country. While the popularity of merrills peaked in Elizabethan times, it was played regularly in homes and farms on the North York Moors until the 1930s, with stable hands drawing up boards on the lids of corn bins and playing by candlelight. Most families would have had a homemade board, usually wooden with a handle, somewhere in the house.

Interest in the game was revived twenty years ago by the Ryedale Folk Museum, which became the home of the World Merrills Association. It staged the first national championships in 1987; this was soon upgraded to become the World Merrills Championships, held annually in mid-September. The last was held in 2002, when the tournament was reluctantly put on ice pending an increase in participants. Boards with instructions are still available for use on site, and are also for sale.

A merrills board has three concentric squares linked through the centre of each side. This provides twenty-four intersection points, on to which the pegs are placed. There are eighteen pegs altogether: nine for each player. The objective is to get three pegs in a row, which creates a 'mill'. On forming a mill, one of the opponent's pieces is removed from the board. The game is won by the player who reduces an opponent's pegs to two, or blocks them from moving. Moves and mills can only be made along the horizontal and vertical lines on the board, never across the diagonal where there are no lines marked. Although the game sounds similar to draughts, it is actually quite different, with three stages of play and a complex set of rules.

While North Yorkshire is among the last bastions of merrills in Britain, the boards have been found in and on historic buildings throughout the world. Traces of boards can be seen on artefacts from the first city of Troy and from a Bronze Age burial site in Ireland. There is a board carved into a roofing slate of a temple in the Nile valley and, in Sri Lanka, a first-century shrine has a board engraved on its steps. Of course, it is impossible to prove that these boards are contemporary with the structures, but the game must have been widely known from very early days. The earliest board that can be accurately dated was found on the Gokstad Viking ship burial of 870.

In Britain, many buildings have boards in positions where play would have been impossible. An assumption is that masons played on the boards before using the stone in construction. In North Yorkshire, one of these stone boards can be seen on a pillar in Pickering Church.

The game has a variety of names in different languages, many relating to 'mill', the term used for three pegs in a row. They include *jeu de moulin* (French), *tavola da molina* (Italian), *seigen wlf myll* (Polish), *mylna* (Icelandic) and *mühlespiel* (German).

Merrrills, the name favoured in North Yorkshire, is derived from Old French and Latin words meaning a counter or playing piece. Another common name in Britain is Nine Men's Morris. In *A Midsummer Night's Dream*, Shakespeare refers to the tradition of playing Nine Men's Morris in the open air, with a board cut into the turf:

The fold stands empty in the drowned field
And crows are fattened with the murrain flock;
The Nine Men's Morris is filled up with mud,
And the quaint mazes in the wanton green
For lack of tread are indistinguishable.

WALK 10

GOATHLAND AND THE ROMAN ROAD

DIFFICULTY 👢👢👢👢 **DISTANCE** 11 miles (18 km)

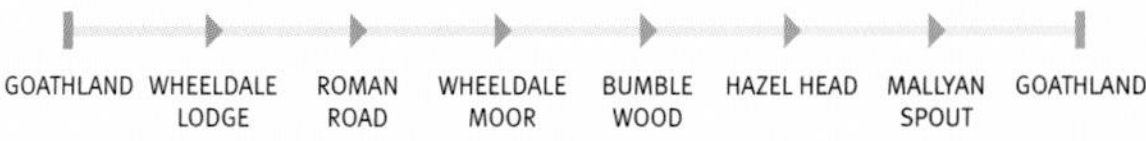

MAP OS Explorer OL27, North York Moors (Eastern Area)

STARTING POINT On the grass verge near the Mallyan Spout Hotel, Goathland (GR 827007)

PUBLIC TRANSPORT North Yorkshire Moors steam railway provides services from Pickering, daily April–October and less regularly in winter (www.northyorkshiremoorsrailway.com; 01751 472508). The Coastliner Leeds–Whitby bus route 840 runs a year-round service (www.yorkshirecoastliner.co.uk; 01653 692556).

PARKING On the grass verge or in the car park at the northern end of the village, near the train station (GR 833013)

This is the North York Moors in a nutshell: moorland, forests, rivers and waterfalls, plus a 'Roman' road and a movie connection. Enjoy the diversity, on a combination of footpaths, bridleways, untracked heather moor and forest tracks.

▶ Start at the southern end of Goathland, at a road junction opposite the Mallyan Spout Hotel, an elegant nineteenth-century country house hotel.

■ Once a remote hamlet on a windswept moor, Goathland is now a television set. Most visitors are on the *Heartbeat* or Harry Potter trails, flocking to a village they know as Aidensfield or Hogsmeade. One reason for Goathland's celluloid fame, and an attraction for many tourists, is the North Yorkshire Moors steam railway, one of the earliest lines in the north of England. The Goathland railway station, familiar to Harry Potter fans, looks the same today as in the nineteenth century.

▶ An open access information board marks the edge of the moor ❶, which this route will cross. An enjoyable line to take is to follow the waymarked bridleway across the flank of the moor, then bear gently left and upwards. Just below a small pond, climb a sunken track that leads to the top of an escarpment and pick up a path that follows the top southwards.

The initial destination is Wheeldale Lodge, a stone house bordered by Scots pines, which

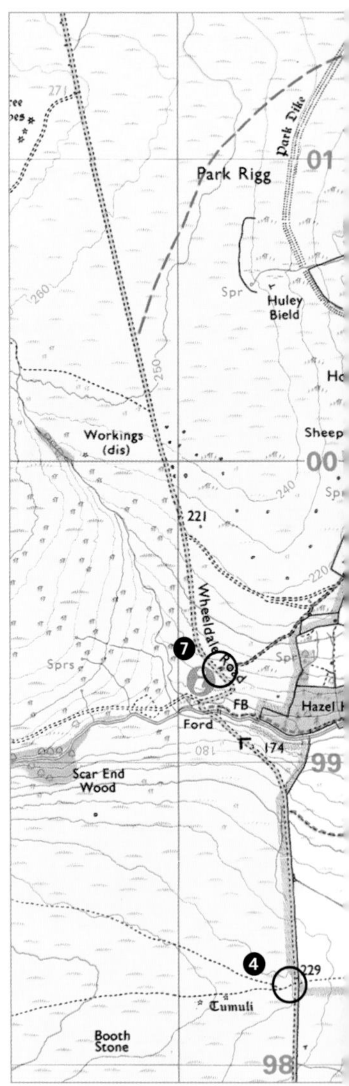

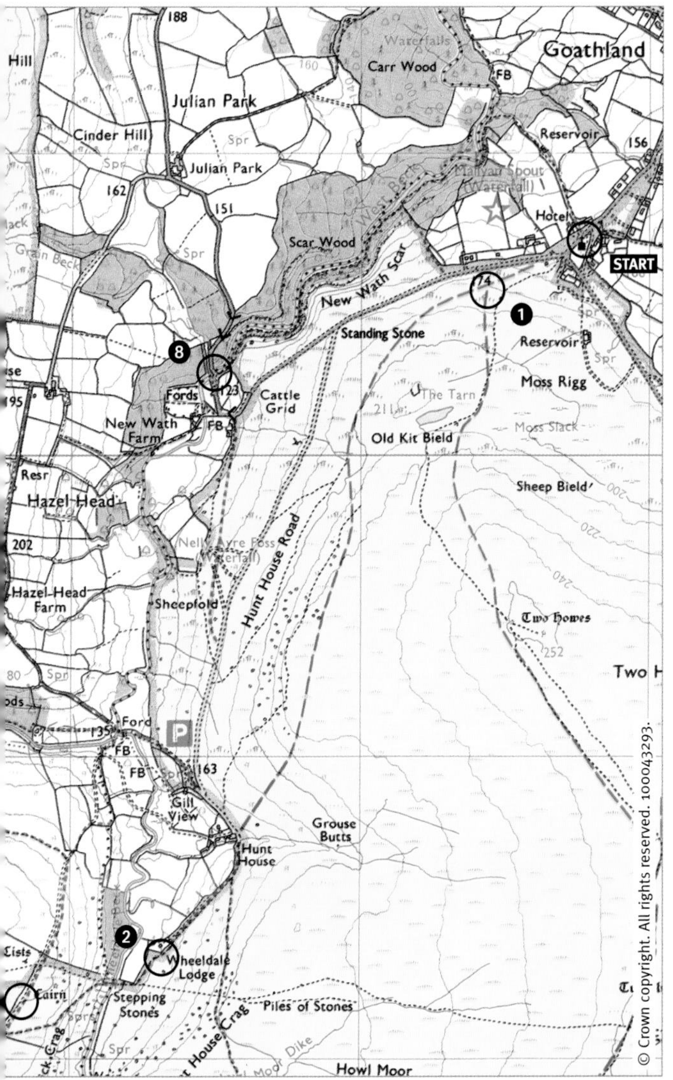

▸ Map continues westwards on pages 120–21

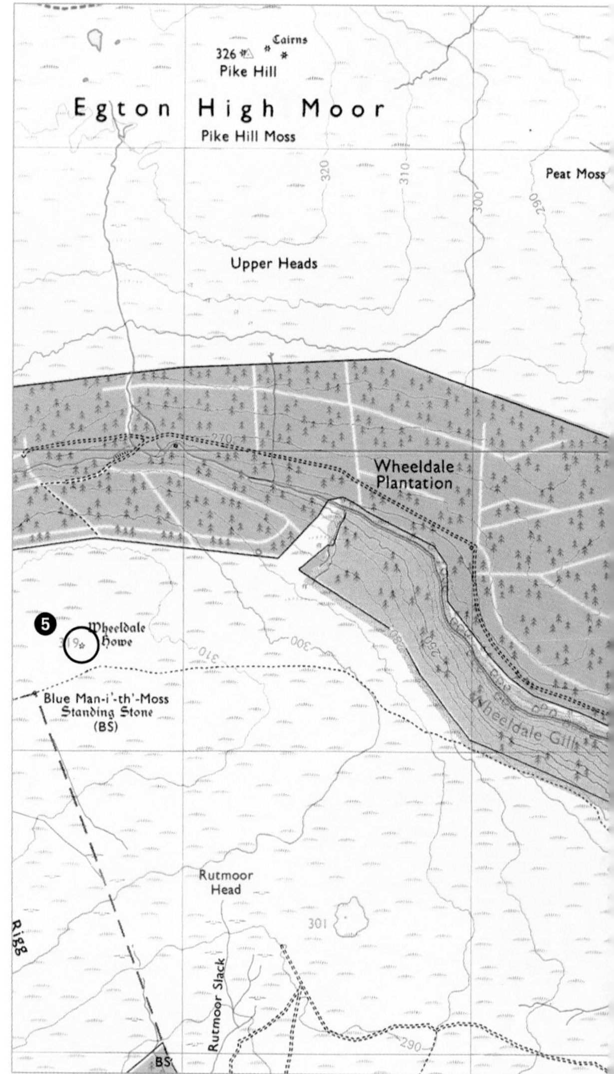
Cairns
326
Pike Hill
Egton High Moor
Pike Hill Moss
320
310
300
290
Peat Moss
Upper Heads
270
Wheeldale Plantation
5
Wheeldale Howe
319
310
300
Blue Man-i'-th'-Moss Standing Stone (BS)
Wheeldale Gill
Rutmoor Head
301
Rigg
Rutmoor Slack
290
BS

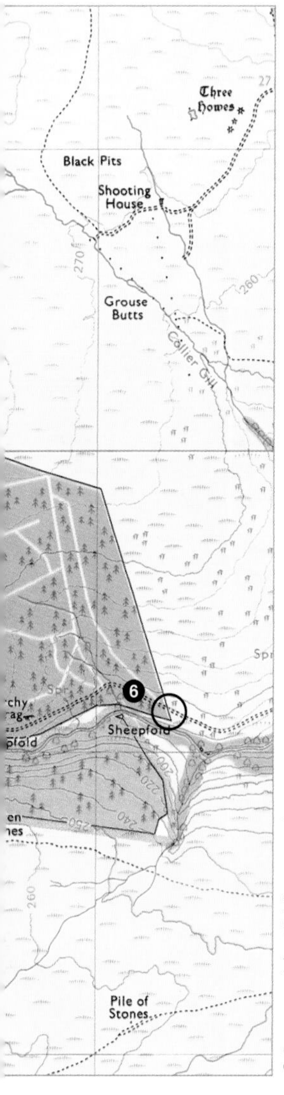

comes into view once the escarpment veers east.

■ This moor is part of the Goathland estate, owned by the Duchy of Lancaster. The 10,340-acre estate has been owned by the Duchy since 1267. It is the Duchy's largest holding in a three-estate portfolio of 17,100 acres within, or on the edge of, the North York Moors National Park.

Founded in the thirteenth century, the Duchy of Lancaster is a unique collection of land, property and other assets held in trust for the Sovereign in his or her role as Duke of Lancaster. Today, the Duchy of Lancaster is custodian of 47,000 acres across England and Wales, including urban developments, historic buildings, high-quality farm land and areas of great natural beauty.

▶ From Wheeldale Lodge ❷ (once a youth hostel but now in private use), follow the footpath to Wheeldale Beck and cross it on neatly spaced stepping stones. Make your way up the far side, straight up the bank or on the footpath that cuts across the hill. At the top is the Roman Road ❸.

■ A stony platform up to 20 ft (6 m) wide in places, the so-called Roman Road runs straight across the eastern edge of Wheeldale Moor. This is its most visible section. Nature has reclaimed some of the foundations which were exposed by archaeologists, but the ditches at either side of the road and the camber can still be clearly seen. Also visible and still in working order are the drainage systems which run across the road.

It was once thought this road connected Cawthorn Roman camp with Whitby and the coastal stations, but expert opinion now is that it may not date to the Roman period after all, or if it does it was built relatively late in the occupation of Britain, when normal Roman road-building standards were not applied. Local legend goes even further, dismissing the Roman connection completely. In this version the road is Wade's Causeway, built by the giant Wade for his wife Bell to herd her sheep to moorland pastures.

▶ To keep on open access land between the Roman Road and the tarmac Wheeldale Road, turn left for a short distance along the Roman Road before crossing the moor. Backtrack north up the tarmac to the crest of the hill and turn left on to Wheeldale Moor on an obvious track ❹.

■ This is the line of the Lyke Wake Walk, a moorland hike of 42 miles (68 km) from Osmotherley on the western side of the moors to Ravenscar on the coast. The first crossing was made in late 1955 in twenty-three hours (thirteen hours walking time). The challenge to complete the walk in twenty-four hours has since been taken up by hundreds of walkers each year. At one time everyone and their

Wheeldale Beck, Goathland

granny (over-sixty-fives are allowed another twelve hours) were attempting the walk, with huge school parties and sponsored groups blundering through the heather. Erosion is now a problem, with peaty sections of the high moors becoming quagmires which are difficult to cross in summer and impossible in winter. The irony is that until open access legislation was passed, much of the walk was not on legal rights of way (indeed some of it remains technically outside open access areas).

▶ Almost immediately the track divides. Take the right fork and follow it over rocks and through heather across and up the moor. At the high point marked on the map as the Blue Man-i'-th'-Moss standing stone, turn right to a large, flat-topped mound known as Wheeldale Howe ❺.

■ There are more than 3000 howes or tumuli on the North York Moors. Burial places of important people from the Middle Bronze Age, they are mostly found on ridges. Howes were often pillaged by Victorian grave robbers for whatever valuable treasure they possessed, but others have been excavated by archaeologists.

▶ From the top of the howe, aim due north towards the forest. At the forest fence turn right to reach a wooden gate. Enter the forest and follow the main track down to a river. Turn right at the junction on the far side, then right again at the next junction, to eventually reach a gate which leads out of the forest ❻.

■ Originally called Wheeldale Plantation, this is one of the largest of the isolated blocks of forest on the open moorland of the North York Moors. In 2005 it was renamed Bumble Wood, a somewhat obscure tribute to the memory of David Arnold-Forster OBE, the former chief executive of the North York Moors National Park Authority.

The renaming is part of a long-term project to revert

the area to broad-leaved woodland and heathland. The Forestry Commission plans to launch a consultation on the new forest design plan, including proposals for felling and restocking with broad-leaved trees. The national park authority has been working with the Forestry Commission and will be funding initiatives to remove conifer regrowth from areas already felled.

▸ The track meets up with the road at the Wheeldale Gill ford, a popular place for picnics and camping. Turn left up the moor to join a footpath heading north-east to Hazel Head ❼. Pick up the bridleway signed for Goathland and follow it through fields and woodland, past New Wath Farm with its plant nursery, to the road. Turn left towards the bridge over West Beck and right on to the footpath up its eastern bank ❽.

■ West Beck, fed by Wheeldale Gill and Wheeldale Beck, flows at the bottom of a deep ravine, with wooded banks rising to the moor. This is a peaceful place, with Mallyan Spout as the focus. A lacy waterfall 70 ft (20 m) high, it cascades over iridescent mossy ledges to the whisky-coloured water below. The waterfall is an understandably popular spot among visitors to Goathland, who rest on the huge boulders at the base before tackling the climb back up to the moor and village.

▸ Once past the waterfall, turn right at the path junction (signed for Goathland) and climb steps up the steep bank to emerge at the Mallyan Spout Hotel.

West Beck, Goathland

The hiss of steam

Pickering is a pretty market town on the edge of the North York Moors. It has a ruined castle, a museum in a fine Regency building and a church with frescos of saints and dragons. Of course, the visitors love these attractions – but they come here for another reason entirely. They flock to Pickering because this bustling town is the terminus for the country's favourite steam railway.

The line, threading through the moors from Pickering to the village of Grosmont, is a magnet for adults and children, walkers and train buffs alike. It stops at unmanned halts, picture-postcard stations, and offers refreshments, scenery and a hug of romance.

The journey starts with a time warp, at Pickering's nineteenth-century station. Advertisement placards from the 1930s cover the walls, milk urns line the platform and the trains, lovingly polished, wait on the tracks. Steam belches as the next departure makes ready – and soon the engine and its carriages grind and chunter away from the town, toward the moors.

Children squeal with excitement as the train eases through the sidings, past tidy allotments, a lake and a barking terrier. The adults grin too – the woman with her video camera, the man in his walking boots, the teenager with a rucksack. They're absorbed in the magic of a lost era, in the feeling of expectation and adventure.

When steam had its heyday, a ride was a journey, not a day trip – but this train can be either. It can be a day out to the upland plateau, to visit the villages and breathe in the steam. Or it can be the start of a walk, long or short, from any of the stations along the way.

Levisham, in scenic Newton Dale, is a popular starting point for short walks in search of wildlife and flowers. Newton Dale Halt is a walkers' request stop, offering longer forays towards the moors. Goathland is the start of our Walk 10, via the Roman Road, and Grosmont is the launch pad for the Rail Trail. The ultimate challenge, and the most enjoyable way of combining steam with a leg-stretch, is to ride the train to Grosmont, then walk back across the moors to Pickering, with an overnight stop in Goathland.

From Pickering the train pushes north, a long, lazy serpent. Steam hangs in the trees, white and swirling like a ghost in a nightshirt. As the train rounds a long corner, passengers lean out of the window. They can see the engine ahead, feel the carriages swaying, smell the steam. Coal grit speckles their faces and trees-stream-horses-woods flash past, in a dizzy blur of movement. The driver pulls the whistle – WHOOOOP – and the engine breathes out, in a great sigh of smoke.

Soon the valley widens to become moorland, and the train arrives in Goathland. The limestone platform reflects a time long gone, with its flowers, milk urns and wicker hampers. Those who scramble for the platform wave at strangers on the train. They're stopping to walk or to explore the settings for *Heartbeat* and Harry Potter, while others on the train continue to Grosmont at the end of the line.

This is the prettiest section, with rivers, woods and moorland grazed to a lawn. Suddenly the engine dives into a tunnel, and out, and arrives with a jolt at the station. It's bustling with guards in blue denim, boys with bikes, families with daypacks and children straining to escape. On an adjacent modern line, the Esk Valley train from Middlesbrough screeches to a stop. No one even glances at it. They're too busy watching the steam train wheeze out its last drops of smoke and prepare for the run back to Pickering.

Some passengers set off on the Rail Trail, along the Murk Esk river back to Goathland. Others explore Grosmont, a moorland village built to house the railway workers and originally called Tunnel. Its steep street and terraced houses have limited appeal and visitors soon make tracks to the locomotive sheds. A short walk through the world's first passenger tunnel, circa 1833, leads to a sign offering a Deviation Shed – a home for restored engines. To get there, the visitors pass Dame Vera Lynn – who proves to be big, black and oily – and a number of signboards giving historical context to the route and its creators.

Who were they? Well, George Stephenson got the ball rolling in 1831 when he surveyed the terrain between Whitby and Pickering. This mission was prompted by a decline in whaling, ship building and alum mining, which led the citizens of Whitby to decide that they needed better land links to the rest of the country.

Stephenson, who was still glowing from his engineering triumphs on the Stockton and Darlington Railway, recommended a railway line with horse-drawn carriages. In 1833 the project commenced, with workers armed with picks and shovels slicing a line through the rough moorland.

The original stretch of 24 miles (39 kilometres) was opened in 1836 and for nearly 130 years trains chugged serenely through the North York Moors. It all came to a grinding halt in 1965 as a result of the Beeching Report, which led to the closure of many lines and stations. The Esk Valley line was saved but the 18-mile (29-kilometre) section of line between Grosmont and Pickering was closed.

Eight years and much hard work later, the North Yorkshire Moors Railway was reopened by a dedicated preservation society. Now it is owned by the North Yorkshire Historical Railways Trust, which has run the line as a living museum since 1974. It has an army of volunteers who, among other things, help organize themed weekends (around themes such as World War II, vintage vehicles or Harry Potter) and special Santa-services at Christmas. Some 30,000 visitors use the service each year.

Today it is the single biggest attraction in the North York Moors National Park. Steam trains (occasionally diesel engines are used but these are clearly indicated in the timetable) operate a full service between March and October, with weekends throughout winter.

Information about the North Yorkshire Moors Railway can be obtained from 01751 472508 (talking timetable 01751 473535) or at www.northyorkshiremoorsrailway.com.

WALK 11

HERITAGE COAST

DIFFICULTY 👞👞👞 **DISTANCE 8 miles (13 km)**

MAP OS Explorer OL27, North York Moors (Eastern Area)

STARTING POINT Beside the A171 Whitby–Scarborough road, at a gate and stile leading on to the west side of Stony Marl Moor (GR 946003)

PUBLIC TRANSPORT Arriva bus 93 from Middlesbrough or Scarborough (www.arriva.co.uk; 0870 6082608) stops at the Flask Inn, 1 mile (1.6 km) from the starting point.

PARKING On the disused road near the starting point (marked 'P' on the OS map)

Snatch a glimpse of North Yorkshire's industrial heritage and enjoy far-reaching views of the sea on this walk over untracked moorland to the Heritage Coast.

▶ From your car cross the A171 and scramble up the bank on the far side. Take a compass bearing of 345 degrees and walk across bare moorland to Cook House Farm. Turn right on to the concrete track along the moor edge. If you are coming from the Flask Inn bus stop, walk south-east down the A171 for just under 1 mile (1.6 km), then turn left down the concrete road to Cook House Farm to reach the same point ❶. Stay on the road, passing a turn-off to Fairview and another to Thorney Brow, where the road becomes a dirt track.

■ This is the first view of North Yorkshire's Heritage Coast. Towering cliffs, sweeping bays and tiny fishing villages make up this historic coastline. Sheltered in narrow ravines, the villages of Robin Hood's Bay, Runswick Bay and Staithes all owe their existence to the fishing industry.

The Jurassic rocks of the Yorkshire coast are famous for their fossils, particularly of dinosaurs. Footprints of these legendary beasts are clearly visible along the shores of Burniston and Scalby. The recent discovery of a

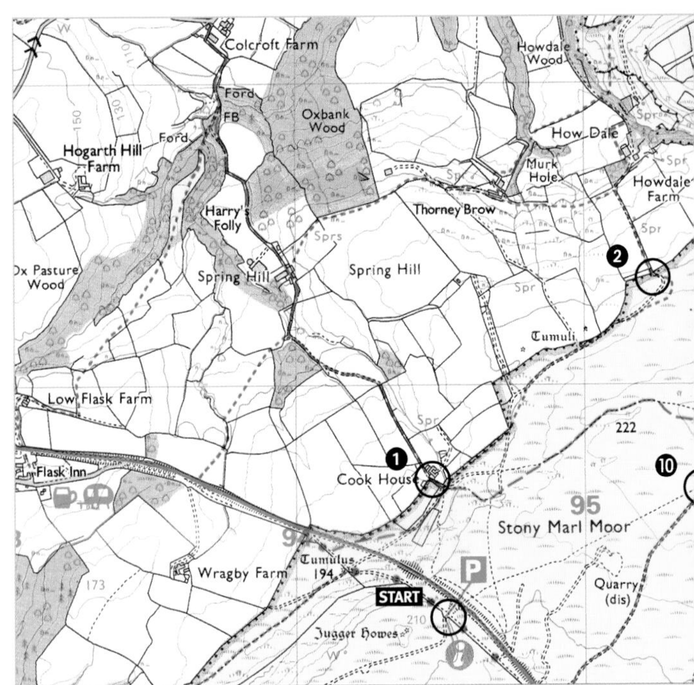

fossilized sea dragon from 132 million years ago has brought the coastline to prominence in scientific circles. The creature, known as a plesiosaur, measured around 15 ft (4.5 m) long and had an elongated neck, a barrel body and four diamond-shaped flippers.

▶ When the track swerves left ❷, continue straight on over the moor, keeping a dry-stone wall on your left. The easiest walking is on the crest of a bank beside the wall. Continue next to the wall, eventually scrambling down to cross a stream. Climb up the far bank and turn left, following the line of the stream.

At a wire-fenced enclosure, turn right and climb the moor. When the fence makes a left turn, continue up to a tumulus on the

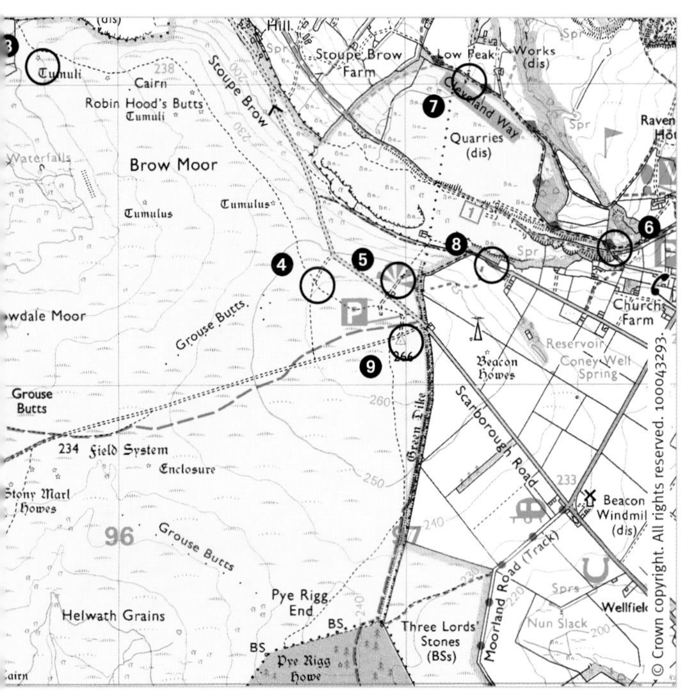

highest point ❸. Then turn right and follow a faint rutted track, which hugs the edge of the Stoupe Brow bank, aiming towards a mast. You will see a tall stone cairn ahead, and at this point the track becomes more definite.

■ From the cairn, look north for a view of Boggle Hole and Robin Hood's Bay. Boggle Hole was thought to be haunted, its name deriving from the 'boggle', or goblin, who was said to live in the area. Now a youth hostel is there, just 100 yards (100 m) from the sea. The hostel was a water mill until 1950, and there are records of a mill's existence on this spot since 1394. The beach and rocky foreshore are fabulous places to hunt for fossils.

Robin Hood's Bay, known to long-distance walkers as the end of the Coast to Coast Walk, is Yorkshire's prettiest seaside village. Its jumble of roofs and white-washed walls, narrow streets and tight-packed houses, seem to be testimony to architectural anarchy. The village, tucked into a crook of the cliffs, is prone to storm damage; in 1780 the main street was washed away and high winds and heavy seas regularly hammer the houses.

The village has a slipway rather than a harbour, and a sandy beach which is inaccessible at high tide. As the only community of any size between Whitby and Scarborough, it was a favoured haunt of smugglers. The Robin Hood connection, however, remains a mystery.

▶ Go straight on when this track meets another, larger track in a T-junction ❹, picking up a faint path over the moor and still heading for the mast. When the path splits, follow the left fork on to a quiet road. Cross the road and walk straight down the moor towards the sea and a fine viewpoint at Ron's Seat ❺. To your right is the windswept village of Ravenscar.

■ Perched on cliffs above the North Sea, Ravenscar, originally known as Peak, is the holiday resort that never happened. In 1890 a developer called John Septimus Bland devised an ambitious plan for a destination to rival Whitby and Scarborough. A station was built, road plans created and drainage installed, but Bland's company went bust and, after thirty years, the plan was abandoned.

Today Ravenscar's main attractions, apart from the incredible views and proximity to superb walking country, are the National Trust Coastal Centre and the Raven Hall Country House Hotel. The hotel was reputedly visited by George III for treatment for madness and melancholia. And before royalty the Romans were here: they built a signal station on the cliffs to relay warnings of invaders to their military bases inland.

▶ From Ron's Seat continue straight down the moor, following a sunken, heather-filled track to meet a bridleway. Turn right along the bridleway and continue as it becomes a track, then a tarmac road. Between Cragg Farm and Church Farm turn left, down a track waymarked as a footpath. Follow the signs down the hill and through a handgate, then turn left on to a footpath and over a small bridge across the disused Whitby–Scarborough railway line.

■ This section of the Whitby–Scarborough coast railway operated between 1885 and 1965. Construction began with the cutting of the first sod in 1872, but by 1878 financial difficulties had set in and the line was temporarily abandoned. It finally opened in 1885, at a cost of nearly £650,000. North Eastern Railway ran the line from the outset, purchasing it in 1898 for just over £260,000.

From 1953, however, stations began to be closed down or left as unmanned halts, and the line was closed for good in 1965. The track was then purchased by Scarborough's forward-thinking council, who used it to create 22 miles (35 km) of permissive footpath and bridleway. A low-gradient route with a highpoint at Ravenscar, much of it runs parallel to the Cleveland Way, which opens up ample opportunity for circular walks.

▶ Turn left on to the Cleveland Way ❻ and descend towards the sea. Follow the path left on to a concrete track, then turn right into the Peak Alum Works. This is the Geological Trail, which makes a loop through the works and then returns to the Cleveland Way.

■ Peak Alum Works, an extensive quarry complex and processing plant, was the largest alum works in Yorkshire and operated from 1650 to 1860. Alum is a crystal containing aluminium sulphate, which is produced by a chemical process and ground into a flour. It was used as a fixing agent in the textile-dyeing industry and as a preservative for tanning leather.

Alum was produced here from shale quarried from the hillside, which was then burned for nine months until the rock went red. The next stage was to soak the rock in water to extract the aluminium sulphate. Materials imported to the site for the production process included stale human urine from Newcastle, apparently collected from buckets left for the purpose on street corners!

The works have been sensitively restored by the National Trust, who acquired the site in 1979. Visitors can also see the remains of the winding engine that hauled heavy loads up from the coast. Watch out for adders in the grass and newts in a small pond on the site.

▶ Continue along the Cleveland Way until the track rises slightly. Turn left over a stile into a field ❼ and climb on a faint grass track (a National Trust permissive footpath) to the railway line. Turn left and follow the broad track to the overhead bridge. Turn right up steps just before the bridge, then right on to the footpath and right again to the

Robin Hood's Bay from Ravenscar

handgate, retracing your steps back to the road.

Turn right on to the road, pass a farm and look for a stile into a field on your left ❽. Climb the hill and emerge on to the moor. Bear left towards the mast, to a vehicle track.

Two bridleway signs point on to the moor. The right sign leads to a track; there should be a white trig point on your left ❾. Continue on this line to the high point of Howdale Moor. Just past the high point, the track swings left. Carry straight on ❿, using a low stone cairn to direct you on to a faint path. Follow this line directly back to the A171 and the start.

Love that llama

Carlos stands with his eyes closed, his breath soft and sweet. Slowly he starts to hum, a low-pitched noise which becomes louder until it whines like a racing car accelerating out of a corner.

A racing car? On the North York Moors? Sound pollution, surely . . . but no one's getting upset about this little outburst. It's coming from a gentleman with shiny eyes, a luxurious fleece coat and a willingness to carry a rucksack – enough good habits to overrule any vocal foibles.

Carlos, as you may have gathered, is a llama. He is part of a team at Wellington Lodge, well placed between the North Yorkshire moorland and its Heritage Coast. His owners, farmers Bruce and Ruth Wright, moved here in the 1990s with their four-legged friends and have built a thriving business by mixing walking with the love of llamas.

The idea is that the llamas carry the lunches and create a soothing ambience, and the walkers walk. That bit's important: llamas have a prominent spine, which could be damaged if a human lump landed on it.

Pretty faces aside, llamas are said to be very quiet, calming creatures; in fact, they're the latest stress-relieving fad in America. Bruce finds this fact hilarious, but says it's true. It must be – it's in print. Wellington Lodge llamas have featured in *Top Gear* magazine, alongside a Saab and a night in a convent, as the ultimate in relaxation.

While Bruce's llamas are unique on the North York Moors, they are a common sight in North America. In addition to offering their soothing services, they have helped the US Forest Service, geologists and engineers get equipment into mountainous terrain, and have also been used as golf caddies.

They are environmentally friendly too: llamas leave no footprints as their large, camel-like pads spread their weight.

They are also very clean, creating communal toilet stops off the track. Inquisitive, alert, keen wildlife spotters and toilet trained . . . walkers, take note, there is a lot to learn from a llama.

As your personal porter, a pack llama provides the ultimate in effortless hiking. One reason is that they carry the rucksacks, and they are also in charge of lunch. Tucked into the panniers of Carlos and his mates, walkers will find a homemade feast of stuffed baguettes, cheese, cake and wine – Ruth is a catering wizard and prepares food for all the treks. Llamas can carry up to 100 pounds (45 kilograms), although the loads are rarely anywhere near that.

All the llamas have different characters, although their famed tendency to spit, Bruce says, is over-rated. Llamas will spit, but only after extreme provocation and rarely at humans.

Their life expectancy is twenty-five years; the most senior at Wellington Lodge is José, born in 1990. He is a broad-beamed grey-and-chestnut fellow who carries his ears flat back and keeps his subordinates in line. He is the lead llama and is obviously Bruce's favourite.

Walking with a llama is nothing like having a dog or even a horse in tow. The first thing you'll notice is the silence. Llamas don't have hooves; they have pads, with two long toenails that look a bit like talons. This arrangement helps them glide gracefully and soundlessly, even on tarmac.

The second surprise is the fact that man and llama are generally eyeball to eyeball. Carlos, for example, is the smallest of the Wellington Lodge llamas and even though he walks with his neck perpendicular to the ground, his head is on a level with that of his human friend.

Bruce says the llamas, which are intelligent creatures, like conversation and he encourages the trekkers to chat to their load-carrying companions. 'If you don't talk to them they think they've done something wrong,' he explains. Each llama has his own fans, and since the inception of Wellington Lodge in 1996 trekkers have come from all over the world to walk with 'their' llama.

Organized treks with llamas run year round, and stretch from morning or afternoon outings to multi-day expeditions. Glaisdale in the heartland of the moors and Roseberry Topping in the north are particular favourites, with routes crossing heather moorland, steep valleys and sections of Roman road. It is a fine sight, indeed, to see South American pack animals tripping lightly along old pannier tracks that were originally built for North Yorkshire pack ponies.

LLAMA LORE

- Llamas usually stand around 4 feet (1.2 metres) tall at the shoulder and weigh 120–170 pounds (55–80 kilograms).
- They are ruminates and have three stomachs.
- Llama hairs have a hollow core for maximum insulation. Because of the long, itchy guard hairs, the fleece is generally used for rugs and panniers.
- The llama was domesticated as a pack animal 10,000 years ago in South America.
- Today they are used in North America to guard sheep, for trekking and as pets and walking companions.
- For more information about the Wellington Lodge llamas, visit www.llamatreks.co.uk.

WALK 12

HOLE OF HORCUM

DIFFICULTY **DISTANCE 8¾ miles (14 km)**

MAP OS Explorer OL27, North York Moors (Eastern Area)

STARTING POINT Hole of Horcum car park on the A169 (GR 854936)

PUBLIC TRANSPORT Buses on the Coastliner Leeds–Whitby route 840/842 stop year round at the Saltersgate Inn (01653 692556; www.yorkshirecoastliner.co.uk).

PARKING In the car park

Explore the Hole of Horcum, with an easy scramble up a miniature canyon, a visit to the legendary Saltersgate Inn and an intimate view of Malo Cross.

▶ Cross the busy A169 from the car park and descend slightly to a track along the rim of the Hole of Horcum.

■ The Hole of Horcum, also known as Devil's Punchbowl, is a spectacular natural amphitheatre scooped out of Levisham Moor. Legend says that the Hole was formed when the giant Wade grabbed a handful of earth to throw at his wife Bell. Reality says, however, that it was created over millennia by glacial meltwater. The Hole has been progressively widened by landslides, which occur when rainwater seeping through porous rock reaches an impenetrable clay layer and is forced back to the surface as a spring. The Hole of Horcum is the centrepiece of Levisham estate, which is owned by the national park authority.

▸ Turn right and walk around the edge of the Hole. Just before a gate on to the open moor, turn left to descend to a stile ❶.

■ The path around the Hole is on an earthwork dyke, which marked a prehistoric boundary. These dykes are common on the North York Moors, and this route passes several of them.

▸ Walk down a deep track to the bottom of the Hole. Leave the footpath before the stream and turn right to make your way over the moor. Aim for a strip of greensward which arrows up the hillside ahead. Climb the track to the top of the hill and turn left ❷, picking your way through heather. Within a few minutes you will cross an ancient dyke running east–west. Pick up a sheep track to continue along the flat ridge top, aiming due south. When the sparse woodland on your left finishes ❸, follow its edge down towards a stream.

■ These few surviving stands of oak, rowan and birch have been fenced off from sheep and, for the first time in centuries, the woodland is expanding. So far 6000 oaks have been grown from locally collected seeds and planted in a project jointly run by the national park and the Forestry Commission.

▸ Stay above the stream on a narrow track, on the edge of the bracken moor. When a wooden footbridge crosses the stream on your left, turn right up a smaller side stream ❹. The stream forks twice: take the left fork, then the right, to enter a narrow rocky canyon called Pigtrough Griff. The bed is dry here, but the sandstone rock can be slippery. Scramble up the canyon, over the lip of a dry waterfall and around fallen tree debris. The rock walls become smaller as you gain height, before the griff peters out on the moor top.

Continue over the heather on the same line as the griff, to meet a wide, well-used footpath ❺. Turn right. The path passes a couple of Iron Age dykes. One is marked with a plaque; turn left here and follow the dyke up the moor ❻.

■ This dyke, a large ditch with two banks, was constructed in prehistoric times, probably to mark the territory of a pastoral family. The earthworks on the near horizon to the east side of the track are part of a fortified farmstead built at a similar time. Ancient enclosures, Bronze Age burial mounds and Romano-British settlements are also dotted across the moor.

▸ The dyke leads to the top of an escarpment. Turn right and follow a path (not marked on the map) along the ridge. This becomes a sunken grass track which deposits you at the foot of the escarpment ❼.

■ It is likely, at this point, that a puff of smoke will waft up from the valley and a breathy whistle will echo across the moor. Steam trains on the North Yorkshire Moors Railway line chug regularly between Pickering and Goathland, and the tiny station of Newton Dale Halt is just below you.

▸ Follow a path which fades and reappears along the base of the escarpment. When it veers right, aim left across the moor towards a large grey pyramid in the distance. This is the Fylingdales early warning radar station.

■ Bleak, windswept Fylingdales Moor seems an unlikely defence hotspot. The Cold War prompted the United States to build an early warning station here, originally in the shape of giant golf balls. These were replaced in the 1990s with the current building, which looks unnervingly like a mega-moorland ghetto blaster. Because of this radar station, Fylingdales Moor is

▸ page 148

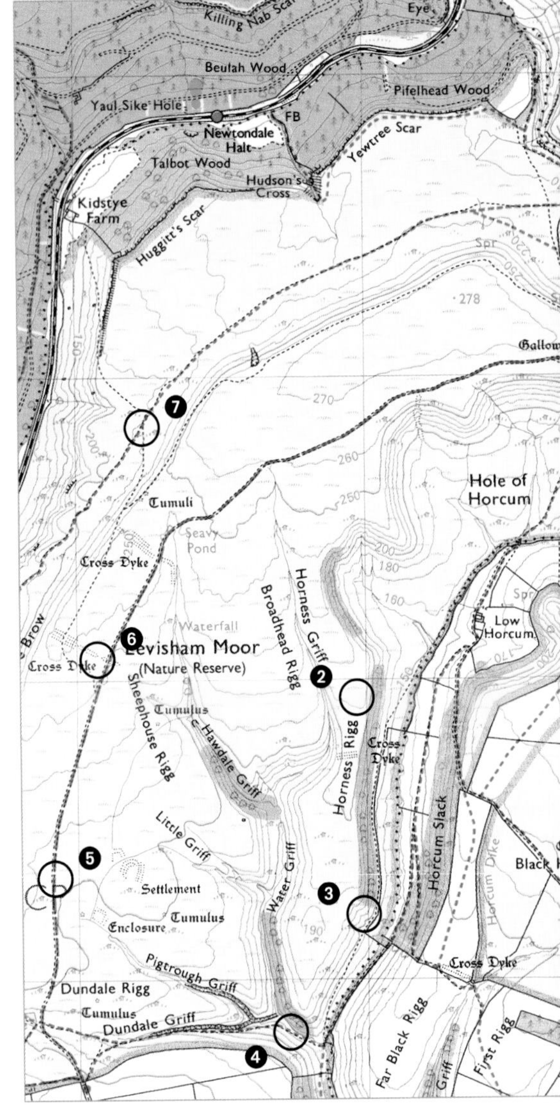
Killing Nab Scar
Eye
Beulah Wood
Pifelhead Wood
Yaul Sike Hole
FB
Newtondale Halt
Yewtree Scar
Talbot Wood
Hudson's Cross
Kidstye Farm
Huggitt's Scar
Spr
278
Gallow
270
260
250
200
180
160
150
Hole of Horcum
Tumuli
Seavy Pond
Cross Dyke
Horness Griff
Broadhead Rigg
Low Horcum
Waterfall
Levisham Moor
(Nature Reserve)
Brow
Cross Dyke
Sheephouse Rigg
Tumulus
Hawdale Griff
Horness Rigg
Cross Dyke
Horcum Slack
Horcum Dike
Little Griff
Water Griff
Black
Settlement
Tumulus
Enclosure
190
Cross Dyke
Pigtrough Griff
Dundale Rigg
Tumulus
Dundale Griff
Far Black Rigg
Griff
First Rigg
1
2
3
4
5
6
7

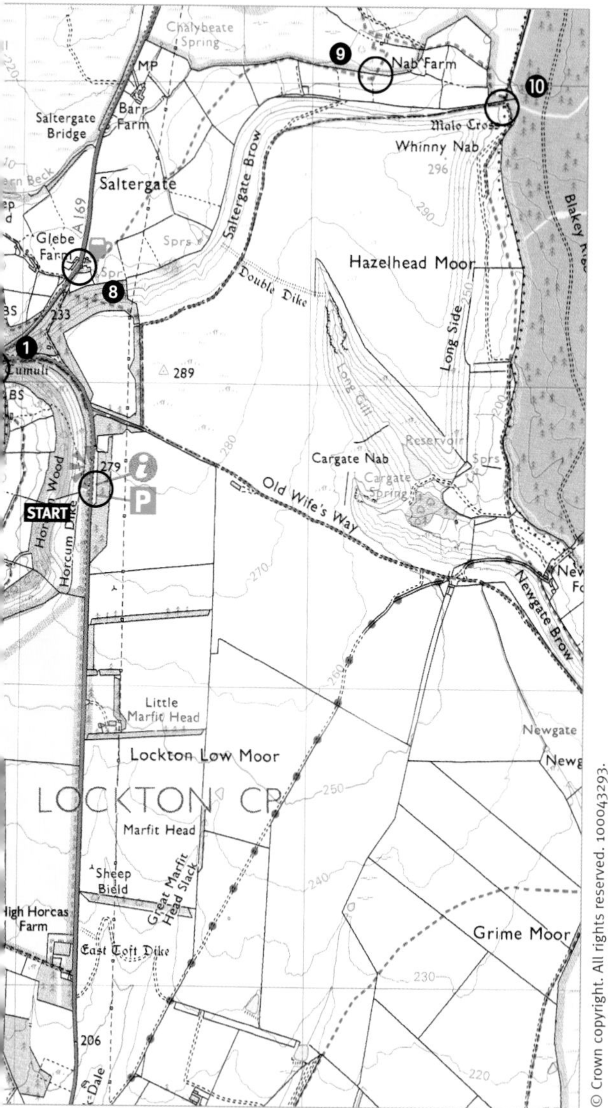
Chalybeate Spring
Nab Farm
MP
Barr Farm
Saltergate Bridge
Malo Cross
Whinny Nab
296
Saltergate
Saltergate Brow
Blakey Rigg
Glebe Farm
Sprs
Hazelhead Moor
Double Dike
233
289
Long Side
Long Gill
Tumuli
Reservoir
Cargate Nab
Cargate Spring
Old Wife's Way
279
START
Horcum Wood
Horcum Dike
Newgate Brow
Little Marfit Head
Newgate
Lockton Low Moor
LOCKTON CP
Marfit Head
Sheep Bield
Great Marfit Head Slack
High Horcas Farm
East Toft Dike
Grime Moor
206

Ministry of Defence property and parts of it are no-go areas for walkers, despite the open access legislation.

▶ Walk down the moor to a gate. Cross the stile and follow the waymarked footpath across fields to the Saltersgate Inn ❽.

■ For the last 270 years, Saltersgate has been known as the inn where the fire never dies. Until the railway was built in 1837, it was the overnight stop for all traffic between Pickering and the coast. Trains of pack ponies were used to transport salt from the salt pans at Whitby to the moorland farms and villages, and the salters used the inn to rest themselves and their animals. A remote place, far from the prying eyes of policemen and customs officers, it was also ideally placed for the salters to ply their second trade: smuggling brandy, tobacco and other highly taxed imports.

The smugglers kept a look-out on the top of Saltergate for those occasions when excise officers did try to approach. On one night in 1730, the officers searched the inn and then departed after, as usual, finding nothing. However, they left one of their number hiding in a farm building. He burst back into the inn to find a contraband auction in full swing, and drew his flintlock to arrest the men. As he did this, a smuggler thumped the officer on the head with a handy oak stool and killed him. The landlord, knowing that his next stop would be the gallows if the body were discovered, buried the officer under the fireplace. On the basis that no one would ever search under a lit fire, he vowed never to let the fire go out . . .

▶ Cross the A169 and climb a high stile over a stone wall. Follow a footpath (not visible on the ground) across fields and along the Saltergate Moor fence line, to a stile facing a stone cottage on the moor ❾. Cross boggy heather to the cottage, turn right and walk along an old stone wall towards a gate and a footpath. Follow the footpath to a junction with a bridleway and the Malo Cross ⓾.

■ Malo is a pretty cross, leaning at a jaunty angle with rounded top and arms. The initials R, E and K, carved on the east face, refer to Richard Egerton, Knight, who set up this cross in the seventeenth century as a boundary stone. For his pains he was accused by the Duchy of Lancaster of trespass. Someone finally took revenge on the beleaguered knight: Malo Cross disappeared for about fifty years before being discovered in a garden in Pickering. It was returned to its position at the foot of Whinny Nab in 1924.

▶ From the cross, follow the bridleway towards the Hole of Horcum, up the side of the nab. Although this looks like moorland, it has enclosed fields so is not open access land. Stay on the bridleway up the bank, across fields, into forestry and back to the car park.

Hole of Horcum

Salt boxes and witch posts

You've walked over a moorland ridge and dropped into a sunny valley. You pass a stone house, maybe with a steeply pitched roof which long ago was thatch. The house is surrounded by a stone wall made of regular blocks of sandstone. But one of the blocks is different. It is hollowed out and in the hole a cat is curled, asleep.

This is the remains of a salt box. Unique to this region, salt boxes were a feature of the old cruck-framed, thatched houses of the moorland. They were made of sandstone, which was easy to find and not difficult to carve, and consisted of an upper and a lower stone. The bottom stone, a square block hollowed out to form a lidless box, was the larger of the two, about 30 inches (75 centimetres) long by 16 inches (40 centimetres) deep. The lid, which was another hollowed-out stone, took the total height of the box to around 22 inches (55 centimetres).

A square hole was cut in the centre of the lid to provide access to the box. Into this space an oak frame was wedged, to which an oak door was attached. The hinges were usually made of leather, which is resistant to salt corrosion, although some were of wood or metal. Once the box was filled the salt could be easily taken out in handfuls, through the door.

The salt boxes were embedded in the thickest part of the wall, which also housed the inglenook fireplace. So, why was the box by the fire? And why in stone? Salt was a precious commodity, used in cooking and as a preservative. It would be bought at intervals, probably from a packhorse train which had travelled from the salt pans at Whitby, and would have to be stored so that it stayed dry. In these old houses, the only place likely to be free of damp was near the fire – and a box made of stone would resist the heat.

Space in this favoured place by the fire was at a premium, however, and used to house bulky cooking utensils such as cauldrons and spits, pots and pans. Setting the stone box into the wall, conveniently close to the cooking pots and the fire, and usually near to the traditional inglenook window (which allowed light to be cast on the cooking), showed a genius for simple design.

Salt boxes are thought to exist in this area because of the proximity of the North York Moors to the coast. Today's A169 between Pickering and Whitby has been called Saltersgate, the salt dealers' road, since the fourteenth century. The salt was transported inland by packhorse or donkey and used for salting meat, fish and butter. Farmers supplied salt beef to sailing ships leaving Whitby for the World Beyond, and their families, snowed into their remote valleys, relied on preserved meat to get through winter.

Tradition is one thing, but nothing is for ever. As the old cruck houses were dismantled to make way for stone houses, the salt boxes were usually thrown out with the rest of the stones. Some were preserved in their original position, but these are rare indeed. Of course, because they were square, many of the boxes that were thrown out were re-used, often finding new homes in garden walls.

Something that did maintain its rightful position in the home was the fireplace. This probably had a smoke hood, tapering up to the chimney, made of wattle and daub or of stone. The smoke hood would have rested on a massive beam, which in turn was likely to have been supported by an oak post carved with an elaborate cross to protect the house from evil.

These ornamented posts were called hecks or witch posts and, apart from one example in Lancashire, are found only on the North York Moors. Because they were part of the house's structure, some of them have been preserved. Examples can be found today in farmhouses in Glaisdale, Egton, Farndale East and Appleton-le-Moors. Rosedale's only known witch post was at Low Bell End; it was removed for use as a gate stop until 1960 and has since been given to the Ryedale Folk Museum.

The witch posts are thought to date from the seventeenth century, although the carving of posts continues a medieval tradition. The markings on one post from Scarborough incorporate signs from astrology, which was a science widely practised in the Middle Ages. Mostly, however, they carry runes invoking the God Thor, protector of the home, or the St Andrew's cross, often carved by the parish priest. They were usually positioned next to the fireplace to prevent evil entering by the chimney.

Witches on the North York Moors apparently had a penchant for turning into cats or hares that could not be stopped except by a silver bullet or a black hound. They put the fear into moorsfolk, but there is little evidence to support their reputation. A rare example of a record from a church court in the seventeenth century shows a Whitby woman accused of bewitching a child to death. There are no details, but perhaps it was her pointy black hat, long nose, wart and razor-sharp fingernails that were the giveaway.

Solitary tree on heather moorland

Some further reading

Here is a small selection of books which will tell you more about the area. Please note that not all are still in print. The website of the North York Moors National Park Authority is www.moors.uk.net.

Margaret Allison, *History of Appleton-le-Moors: A Twelfth-Century Planned Village*, self-published, 2004

Bill Breakall, *Old Pannier Tracks*, North York Moors National Park, 1982

Paul Hannon, *Cleveland Way Companion*, Hillside Publications, 1989

Marie Hartley and Joan Ingilby, *Life and Tradition in the Moorlands of North-East Yorkshire*, Smith Settle, 1990

R. Hayes, *A History of Rosedale*, North York Moors National Park, 1987

R. Hayes and J. Hurst, *A History of Hutton le Hole*, North York Moors National Park, 1989

R. Hayes and G. Rutter, *Rosedale Mines & Railway*, Scarborough Archaeological and Historical Society, 1991

John Morrison, *Ordnance Survey Leisure Guide: North York Moors*, AA Publishing, 1999

Elizabeth Ogilvie and Audrey Sleightholme, *An Illustrated Guide to Crosses on the North Yorkshire Moors*, Village Green Press, 1994

Royal Commission on the Historical Monuments of England, *Houses of the North York Moors*, HMSO, 1987

Peter Simcock, *Rock Climbs on the North York Moors*, Cleveland Mountaineering Club/Cordee, 1985

The Countryside Code

An abbreviated version of the Countryside Code, launched in 2004 and supported by a wide range of countryside organizations including the Ramblers' Association, is given below.

Be safe – plan ahead and follow signs
Even when going out locally, it's best to get the latest information about where and when you can go; for example, your rights to enter some areas of open land may be restricted while work is being carried out, for safety reasons or during breeding seasons. Follow advice and local signs, and be prepared for the unexpected.

Leave gates and property as you find them
Please respect the working life of the countryside, as our actions can affect rural livelihoods, the safety and welfare of animals and people, and the heritage that belongs to all of us.

Protect plants and animals, and take your litter home
We have a responsibility to protect the countryside now and for future generations, so make sure you don't harm animals, birds, plants or trees.

Keep dogs under control
The countryside is a great place to exercise dogs, but it's every owner's duty to make sure their dog is not a danger or nuisance to farm animals, wildlife or other people.

Consider other people
Showing consideration and respect for other people makes the countryside a pleasant environment for everyone, whether they are at home, at work or at leisure.

Index

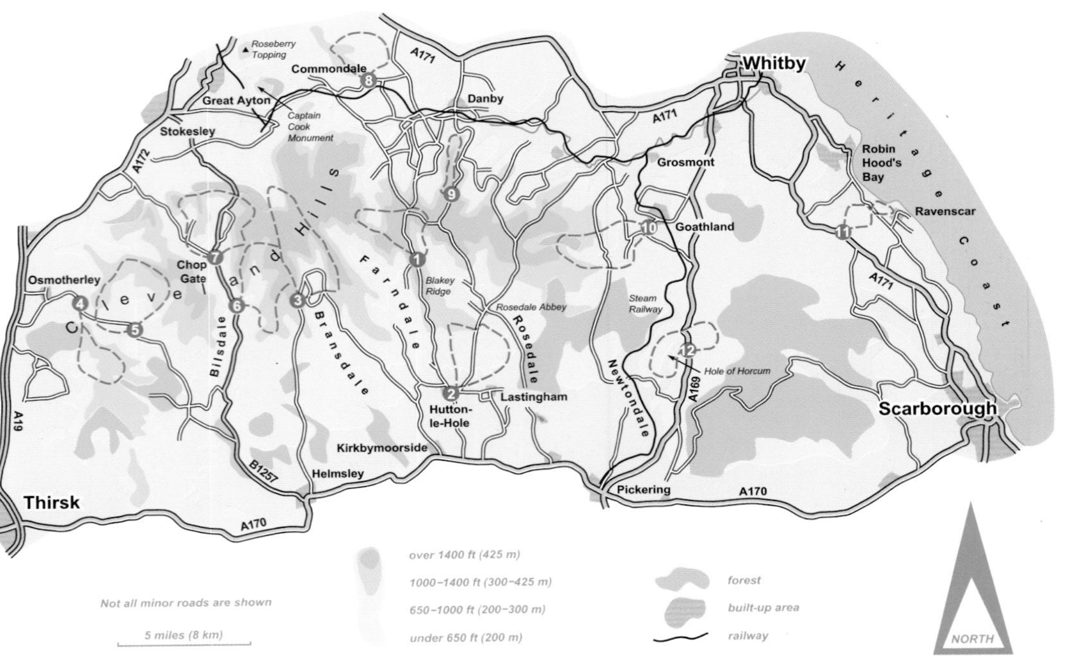

Roseberry Topping
Commondale
Great Ayton
Captain Cook Monument
Stokesley
A172
A171
Danby
Whitby
Heritage Coast
Robin Hood's Bay
Ravenscar
Grosmont
Goathland
Cleveland Hills
Farndale
Blakey Ridge
Rosedale Abbey
Rosedale
Steam Railway
Hole of Horcum
A169
Newtondale
Osmotherley
Chop Gate
Bilsdale
Bransdale
Hutton-le-Hole
Lastingham
Scarborough
Kirkbymoorside
Helmsley
B1257
Pickering
A170
Thirsk
A19
1
2
3
4
5
6
7
8
9
10
11
12
Not all minor roads are shown
5 miles (8 km)
over 1400 ft (425 m)
1000–1400 ft (300–425 m)
650–1000 ft (200–300 m)
under 650 ft (200 m)
forest
built-up area
railway
NORTH